GOOD BUT NOT GOOD ENOUGH

GOOD BUT NOT GOOD ENOUGH

HER DREAM, HIS WORLD

SIMRAN SAHOO

MANUSCRIPTS
PRESS

GOOD BUT NOT GOOD ENOUGH
Her Dream, His World

ISBN   979-8-88926-762-1   *Paperback*
         979-8-88926-763-8   *Ebook*

To my mom, dad, grandmother, and Khusi—thank you for not only providing me endless opportunities but staying by my side through them too.

Contents

Introduction

With a childhood plagued by nightmares and genuine fear of sleep—because I was scared to confront what I would find there—I searched tirelessly for a sweeter getaway from the world. The recurring visions that kept me awake at night uncannily resembled the plot of a horror movie: Night after night, I found myself racing down the same trail ablaze with fire as a murderer with bloodstained teeth chased me. So, if my dreams were tainted with such darkness, at least I could turn to the world inside my pages for comfort.

I was the kid who read fiction under my desk while everyone poured over their history textbooks and pretended not to hear me try to flip the page discretely. In the dead of winter, when other kids were catching snowflakes with their tongues, I was forcing friends to sit on the slushy blacktop and read *The Babysitters Club* together. And on our weekly trips to the library, I would push everyone out of the way so I could be the line leader and escort my classmates there.

Fairy tales, mystery books, romance novels, dramatic plays, and even picture books if I had an especially bad day—I read anything I could put my hands on. There was one exception, though. I refused to venture to the library's non-fiction aisle. In my five years at Exton Elementary School, I checked out exactly one non-fiction book, and it was for a school project. In complete honesty, I do not think I even read it.

To me, a book was only worth reading if the author had created a new reality, one with characters they colored in while sipping steaming hot coffee and brainstorming an entire universe out of the same twenty-six letters everyone has access to but that they somehow rearranged differently. I didn't understand why I should read a book on the unique properties of rocks when there were hundreds of stones scattered in my backyard or open a biography featuring Albert Einstein when my pinky was already poised to click on his Wikipedia.

I am sixteen years old now. Although reading has unfortunately become an afterthought because of my busy days, it will be something I will always hold close to my heart. Yet, I recognize the immaturity my younger self held. I hid from the world in a tiny bubble I had created to protect myself because I was petrified to accept reality. I boasted that I had traveled everywhere from Neverland to Oz when I really sat in the corner of my bedroom, completely stationary for six hours with my nose buried into a creased book. I refused to learn about my surroundings. I ran away from the five o'clock news channel every evening because the stories of gunshots, crying children mourning the loss of their mothers, and floods wiping out entire towns reminded me there is evil in this world too.

However, I believed that if I chose to ignore our universe's horrors, I could continue living the fairytale I wanted everyone's lives to embody. I spent so much of my childhood fearing scary creatures in the darkness with me, not realizing my avoidance of the real world made me more susceptible to being completely alone—which was arguably more frightening.

So, I find it slightly ironic how I am sitting here without a cup of coffee (I am too scared I will become addicted to the beverage) and choosing to *write* a non-fiction book.

All the stories I grew up with had happy endings, but I am old enough to realize now that my own story might not have one.

I remember in sixth grade, for a local speech and debate competition, I sat down to write a piece about female superheroes in our world only to uncover a discouraging editorial by a man expressing how frustrating it was for him to have to work with a woman because they were just so "dumb" and "sensitive." As I read the attached comments—which seemed to multiply by the hundreds, all expressing agreement to the original post—I realized every woman is a superhero, whether they find the treatment for cancer or hold their head high even as another person tries to belittle their worth.

Here's what I didn't understand: In my days of reading fairytales, I was told that I, a little girl, could do anything I wanted as long as I worked hard. I believed them. But when we little girls grow up, we will realize we live in a world riddled with gender inequality—especially in the workplace. We will have to scream louder than our male coworkers to be heard through the same megaphones. We will go to work before the sun rises and come home after it sets only to be left standing in the dark, demanding the same pay as the man who only showed up every other afternoon. We will be forced to bite back tears as other men continually make us feel worthless.

Some might give up.

I am afraid I will. Can I, the same girl who checked the closet doors seventeen times to ensure no monsters were around before she slept, stand her ground against real-life monsters? I am scared I will give everything I have to everything I do, then be undermined because I might be grown but, to everyone else, I will seem like a starry-eyed girl who got lost in someone else's reality. That I will be *good* but not *good enough*.

After having the privilege of meeting incredible women who have gone through everything described above and more, I know that I can make it. Their stories of inspiration, built on the pain and struggles they endured, will forever act as a guiding light to support me through whatever battles I may have to overcome in the future. Their perseverance inspires me to work even harder, because I know now that when people attempt to discourage me, they cannot take away my courage.

We can form all the amazing friendships we want with the fictional characters we meet in books—but we also have to recognize the struggles and accomplishments of seemingly ordinary people who have gone through unimaginable things in their lives and were resilient. They didn't give up.

They had dreams too. Some were fulfilled. Some weren't. But these women were all heroes in their own stories.

I am far from a hero. I am a high-school student with big dreams. But I have been creating a portfolio of research regarding workplace gender inequality for the past five years, writing speeches for original oratory competitions and even spoken-word poetry regarding the topic. There is so much discouragement present in those statistics and testimonials, so I wanted to create a permanent piece of writing that instead motivates women to see the bravery and light this world possesses even in the darkness of inequality. I was exhausted from wondering if the dreams I had spent my childhood forging would ever come true because I was a girl. And as I looked around and saw all the women surrounding me, I felt indignant on their behalf that they ever had to endure such unbearable pain for a factor they had no control over.

If I recognize how frustrating it is that we kids grow up together, share the same toys in preschool, read the same books during circle time, and spend the same amount of time on our homework, only to be separated in the future by something the boys called "cooties," then so can others my age (and hopefully older). A common misconception is that workplace gender inequality only affects women, but I want to remind everyone that those women were once little girls with big aspirations too—just like me.

The idea of "success" no longer appeals to me if not everyone can share in the joy of it. After all, when these women struggled to overcome discrimination, they weren't just fighting for themselves—but for us, the younger generation. Their battles are our war too. And that war is yours whether you are a girl, boy, woman, man, or beyond. When women succeed, everyone succeeds. I write this book now, though, for my generation: to show them how far women before us have come and how far we have left to go.

This book will be in the non-fiction aisle, and I know my little self would never have picked it up, but I wish I had read a story like this one when I was younger. I think I would have grown up to look at the world with much braver eyes.

Chapter 1

Progress. For me, I do not equate progress with success. As I began writing this book, I found myself looking beyond the journey and obstacles and the distance I traveled. The grounds I uncovered and battled for were lost to me if I did not *achieve* the goal I set out to complete. I have lost track of the number of experiences at which I failed, whose lessons I threw away because the thought reminded me of my painful, unbearable lack.

Prior to my research, I knew nearly nothing about women's history and that knowledge was limited to only their present obstacles. As my research uncovered more and more workplace horror stories, I thought writing this book would only emphasize the struggles women have endured. Then I realized my ignorance. While acknowledging the gender inequality still present in our society is crucial, we must also appreciate how far we *have* come.

When I began looking into female historical heroes, I realized so much of my inspiration for taking on this project was out of anger and frustration that in the twenty-first century, women still struggle for equal treatment in the workplace. I continually questioned how, in a time where we have self-driving electric vehicles, automated robots that can vacuum entire houses, and virtual reality glasses, we can still blatantly mistreat and hurt female employees. It bothered me that we have so much creative intelligence and brainpower in this world—but not near enough respect.

Though the gap in opportunities for women now is much less pronounced, it was once more significant. Our ancestors fought for basic common rights. They pioneered breaking away from traditional gender stereotypes, and their contributions paved the way for us women today. This is our opportunity to pick up the mantle and be their voice to fight against discrimination.

The story begins with Abigail Adams, wife of the second US president, John Adams. She pleaded earnestly in a letter to him: "I desire you would remember the ladies, and be more generous and favorable to them than your ancestors. Do not put unlimited power into the hands of the husbands. Remember, all men would be tyrants if they could. If particular care and attention is not paid to the ladies, we are determined to foment a rebellion, and will not hold ourselves bound by any laws in which we have no voice or representation" (Adams 1776). She wanted him to think of women and their wishes when he and his governmental panel sat down to draft the new laws and rules that would govern America (Adams 1776).

Unfortunately, Adams did not take his wife's letter seriously and instead replied with, "As to your extraordinary code of laws, I cannot but laugh. […] We know better than to repeal our Masculine systems," disregarding the First Lady's opinions as saucy and impractical (Adams 1776). John Adams was a firm believer that with the political chaos clouding the late 1700s, especially with America establishing our constitution, changing the logistics of voting or other male-dominated activities would be unwise.

He also was a proponent of many men's mindsets during this time: that women were far too reliant on their husbands to be able to form their own determinations and exercise the right to be involved in decision-making. A person, in his eyes, could only have independence if they owned their own property. Since that privilege was granted only to white men, he believed women and other disenfranchised demographics such as African Americans did not deserve to make their own decisions (Mandresh 2022). Abigail Adams, still, was one of the very first voices for women's involvement in government, despite most men surrounding her harboring a contradictory mindset. In fact, Adams joined Judith Sargent Murray's movement to broaden women's educational opportunities because she fervently believed in the responsibility women held in building future generations of passionate and virtuous leaders (Michals 2015).

Progress. It is truly mind-boggling. Two hundred and forty-seven years ago, Abigail Adams implored her husband to cast away tradition and include women in driving American democracy, and now in the 2020s, we have surpassed her vision. I wonder what her reaction would be if she knew that instead of only a First Lady, there is now also a female vice-president in office.

The lack of feminine involvement, however, was emphasized in the workforce as well. Up until 1847, every single graduate of a medical university was a man. Initially, Elizabeth Blackwell, who would become the first female doctor, was severely averse to the idea of being in the medical field too. It wasn't until after an encounter with a close family friend, who was on her deathbed after battling uterine cancer with the aid of only male doctors, that she slowly began to consider putting aside her aversion to medical books and serve people (Heyn n.d.). After all, her friend had told Blackwell, "If I could have been treated by a lady doctor, my worst sufferings would have been spared me" (Heyn n.d.).

Blackwell sent applications to more than twenty medical colleges, only to receive rejection letters from them all. She was lucky enough, however, to have a male physician write a letter to a college for her, but the status of her acceptance lay in the hands of the entire medical class who were asked to vote on the matter. They, jokingly, said yes—but Blackwell arrived at the campus nevertheless, determined to prove her worth and graduated at the top of her class, aspiring to become a surgeon (Heyn n.d.).

Unfortunately, this dream was extinguished when Blackwell lost the use of her left eye after accidentally splashing fluid into her pupil while operating on a baby's infected eye in a maternity hospital. While she could no longer be a surgeon, she instead opened up her own clinic called the New York Dispensary for Poor Women and Children, where she provided health care completely free to those who were unable to afford it. In 1857, she founded another infirmary, this time for indigent women and children, which was entirely run and operated by female surgeons and workers. Ten years later, she established the Women's Medical College of the New York Infirmary to offer women with medical degrees a facility to develop their skills through practical, hands-on experience (Heyn n.d.).

Progress. Blackwell was motivated enough to pursue her dream of being a doctor and save people's lives. But her true contributions lie in her efforts to make that dream possible for many other women by creating organizations to support their health care endeavors.

Around this time, two other passionate women, Lucretia Mott and Elizabeth Cady Stanton, banded together for women's rights, specifically suffrage, after they were refused a spot on the convention floor at the 1840 World Anti-Slavery Convention. These two women, along with three others—Martha Wright, Mary Ann McClintock, and Jane Hunt—organized their own multi-day convention where they would discuss the "social, civil, and religious condition and rights of women" at Seneca Falls. The first day was designated solely for women (History.com Editors 2017).

Stanton presented the Declaration of Sentiments and Grievances, which the five had drafted, to the women who came—a document bearing close resemblance to the Declaration of Independence. But, crucially, they added the phrasing, "We hold these truths to be self-evident: that all men and women are created equal; that they are endowed by their Creator with certain inalienable rights" to make the text more inclusive. The second day, revolutionary male abolitionists such as Frederick Douglass attended. The ninth resolution, which stated that women deserve the right to vote, received heated debate. After much discussion, the women and men present passed twelve specific resolutions pertaining to women's rights (History.com Editors 2017).

Two weeks after this meeting, the larger Seneca Falls Convention was held with a wide group of people in attendance—but was met with great opposition. In fact, many previous supporters of women's rights decided to pull back from defending the issue. However, many men, such as the editor of the *New York Tribune*, expressed that while they were wary of women voting, they believed if America had to follow the constitution, then they must give women the same opportunities as men (History.com Editors 2017).

In 1869, Stanton and another renowned figure, Susan B. Anthony, created the National Woman Suffrage Association after the Fifteenth Amendment, which allowed African American men to vote, had been passed. The NWSA were severely opposed against this amendment, furious that the right of suffrage had not been granted to them first, and demanded to be heard on the Congress floor. During this time, the American Woman Suffrage Association was also formed and were in direct opposition to the NWSA's accusatory tone towards the Fifteenth Amendment despite sharing the common goal of voting privileges. Their main course of action was to slowly have women be able to vote on matters at the local and state levels before building up to national action.

Slowly, the two organizations merged in 1890, becoming the National *American* Woman Suffrage Association (or NAWSA). Together, they created unique tactics that would bring national attention to the issue of suffrage. Susan B. Anthony decided to take a courageous step and vote in the 1872 New York election—and was arrested for "knowingly, wrongfully, and unlawfully voting," as well as charged with a $100 fine (that she refused to pay). These strategies became bigger, transforming into large, showy parades with thousands of women marching down streets and waving banners in their hands. Another woman's organization, called the National Woman's Party, conducted a White House picket in silence for six days a week over the span of three years, even as many participants were carted off to jail (US National Archives and Records Administration 2021).

Although suffrage had not been implemented nationally, individual states began slowly adopting the measure. Jeannette Rankin, who grew up with six sisters, knew the power of women. She began as a student volunteer in Washington State, helping develop a suffrage campaign that eventually led to her work as a field secretary with NAWSA. On one of her work trips to Montana, she overheard that a woman's suffrage resolution would be introduced and eagerly went to the statehouse to supervise the legislation process. However, she was disappointed to hear this resolution was simply an elaborately orchestrated hoax. Rankin immediately leapt into action, persuading a lawmaker to still introduce the resolution, and in February she stood in front of the Montana legislature and supported women's suffrage. Her testimony spurred the majority of the house to validate the measure, and after continued work there, suffrage was eventually made state law in November of 1914 (History, Art and Archives n.d.).

Recognizing Rankin's value, NAWSA sent her to different areas around the country, some notable ones being Ohio, Florida, and Michigan. Rankin's contributions allowed her to continue making a more pronounced difference in Montana's community, and she decided to finalize her intent to run as a Republican to hold the position of one of two at-large, federal House seats. She ran on a campaign of several important issues to her, such as national suffrage, child welfare, and alcohol prohibition.

Combined with familial support and her previous experience garnering support for unpopular ideas, Rankin was able to secure the position, becoming the first woman to join the nation's federal congress as a representative—undoubtedly because of support she gained from other women she had empowered to vote. In fact, she said in a speech, "I am deeply conscious of the responsibility, and it is wonderful to have the opportunity to be the first woman to sit in Congress. I will not only represent the women of Montana, but also the women of the country." Rankin took this responsibility very seriously, becoming the "Ranking Member" of a new suffrage committee when it was established in 1917, and imploring her colleagues to explore the question of how this country could possibly be a safe democracy when half the population was denied voting power (History, Art and Archives n.d.).

Rankin, as well as notable figures from other organizations, pressed the issue of suffrage from several different angles. After New York joined in on expressing its support for women's suffrage, the President at the time—Woodrow Wilson, who was initially wary about backing women's right to vote—decided to change his mind. Now these groups had garnered the necessary political support, and public outrage tipped the scale in women's favor.

The Nineteenth Amendment, which stated the right to vote shall not be denied or abridged by the state on account of sex, had been introduced at every federal Congress session for forty-two years but was ignored or struck down each time. In 1919, it was finally ratified with states such as Illinois and Michigan leading the way (US National Archives and Records Administration 2021).

Progress. The fight for suffrage was not won by just one group of people but rather multiple waves of women from different backgrounds. It is frightening to think there was once a time when women were unable to engage in their nation's most important decisions, and it is even more inspiring to realize how much time and energy was spent overturning those notions.

A few years after women's suffrage passed, Nellie Tayloe Ross made her debut into US politics—first as her husband's wife. At the time, her husband, William B. Ross, was the Democrat Governor of Wyoming. Ross used her charming personality to make connections with others within the community, then after her husband died in October of 1924, Ross began entertaining the idea of replacing him as governor.

She felt called to finish the work he had started, especially since she helped develop them during his tenure as governor. Most importantly, Ross was excited to see what differences she could make. Yet, the social environment gave her trepidation. If she ran and lost, any jobs being offered now by sympathetic Republicans who helped her support her family might be taken away. Most importantly: in the 1920s, Wyoming was a predominantly Republican state, much like it is today, with many people holding the belief that "governorship was a man's job" (Rea 2014; McFarland 2022).

On January 5, 1925, after her ardent woman supporters and friends pushed for her election bid, Ross was inaugurated into office as the nation's first female governor. It was a true testament to her resilience, as she was thrust into a rough political environment with droughts, bank failures, property loss, oil decline, and deadly mine explosions enshrouding Wyoming (Rea 2014). Although many believed that Ross could not possibly stomach all these issues with her "fragile" femininity, she dove headfirst into work, creating stricter regulations for coalmines, providing loans to farmers, and requiring budgets for districts and cities.

Ross also used her position to interact with other women, giving speeches to different women's organizations such as the Woman's National Democratic Club and the Woman's World Fair. She proudly voiced she did not represent the type of politician that "violated their sense of what the Lord intended a woman should be." Despite losing her re-election bid, she was still able to further her political career, becoming the first woman to ever hold the position of Director of the Bureau of the Mint (Rea 2014).

Progress. As the first female governor of Wyoming, Ross did not just prove herself worthy enough to be in political power—she proved that every woman is capable of being a political leader (Rea 2014). Her resilience gave hope to other women with similar ambitions that it *can* be done.

I yearn for gender equality in our society. I long for a day that the way we are treated in our careers is not dictated by our femininity and that the dreams we want to fulfill are not hindered by the "wo-" part of our gender identity. But I am wary if our society will ever get there. The centuries-old stigma in our world cannot be destroyed, but it can be diminished—and these women dedicated their lives to make more progress. The story, however, does not end with Ross. It continues long after the 1950s.

Chapter 2

On February 19, 1963, Betty Friedan overturned the pre-existing notion that women were content and satisfied with the domestic lifestyle and living out the perfect "American Dream," consisting of marrying a man and having children with him (Muñoz 2021). She published the book *The Feminine Mystique*, which discussed how although women had come a long way from the 1800s, they were still severely weighed down by American societal standards. She used primary accounts from housewives who underscored how their lives—from birth to death—had been reduced to solely taking care of the house and raising children. Even the education system, women's magazines, and advertisements were just reminders the female image was built by men to be seen as secondary and less than (History.com Editors 2019).

Progress. Her book allowed for the suppressed thoughts many women had kept inside of them for so long to be finally spelled out on paper. The work helped start feminism's second wave, in which issues such as equal pay and legalizing abortion access for women were further tackled. Her book, however, did face great criticism from women who believed she was "hysterical" for daring to say women were not content with their household duties. Others noticed how Friedan only painted the struggles of straight, married, white women and did not include anyone else in her scope (History.com Editors 2019).

In 1969, Dr. Bernice Sandler—who as a little girl vowed to her mother she would "change the world" and grew up watching teachers delegate all classroom activity responsibilities to the boys—was working at the University of Maryland when she made a bid to move from her current part-time position as a teacher to full-time (Goldman and Chappell 2019). But there were only seven spots open, and Sandler, unfortunately, did not receive one of them. When she questioned one of the faculty members about why she was not able to secure this position, he responded that although "her qualifications were excellent," her application was ultimately rejected because she "came on too strong for a woman" (Goldman and Chappell 2019). Her response was not as strong: She returned home with a heavy heart and sobbed.

Her gender was the reason she was turned away for two more jobs, with people citing she was "just a housewife who went back to school." But, inspired by stories of other women who had been barred from working or receiving an education, Sandler thoroughly researched legal texts and found a footnote in Executive Order 11246, which President Lyndon B. Johnson had amended to say that discrimination based on sex was illegal—outlawing it in colleges and universities as well (Goldman and Chappell 2019). Inspired by this discovery, Sandler created partnerships with the Women's Equity Action League and helped provide research and statistics about women in academia. She also aligned with congress-members such as Representative Martha Griffiths of Michigan and, most importantly, Representative Edith Green of Oregon.

Progress. Green and Sandler worked together to hold congressional hearings and draft a bill that would eventually come to be Title IX of the Education Amendments. On June 23, 1972, President Nixon signed their legislation into law. Now, "no person in the United States shall, on the basis of sex, be excluded from participation in, be denied the benefits of, or be subjected to discrimination under any education program or activity receiving federal financial assistance" (US Department of Health and Human Services 2921). Because of Title IX, 16,500 school districts and 7,000 post-high school establishments, charter schools, public schools, libraries, museums, and athletic teams can no longer use gender as a motivating factor in their decision to reject someone, as it was in Sandler's case (US Department of Health and Human Services 2021).

Though a variety of work-related opportunities were being opened to women in the 1970s, a very subtle way of regulating their newfound freedom from the money they earned was in place: Unmarried women were not allowed to have their own lines of credit, and if they wanted to open one they had to have a spouse cosign (El Issa 2020). This was due to the pervasive male view that women did not have the intelligence or capability to manage their own finances. Banks, in particular, believed that lending credit to a woman was too large a risk. An unmarried woman could wake up every day and go to work—but did not possess the privilege of transferring that money onto a credit card for ease of use. Even if a woman was married, though, they should still have been able to independently open credit to protect them in case something happened to their husband (Pham 2021).

Progress. In 1974, after protests from several women's organizations regarding blatant financial inequality, the Equal Credit Opportunity Act passed, which forbade credit card companies to use gender, religion, race, or national origin as a reason to deny someone credit (ECOA 1974).

Before all this, though, the finance realm saw the fiery passion of Isabel Benham. She entered the world insistent on pursuing education instead of taking on secretarial or domestic tasks, and in 1931 became one of only five women to leave college with an economics degree. Still, her degree was not enough to compensate for her gender, and finding a job was difficult, especially in the midst of the Great Depression. When she mentioned wanting to seek a career on Wall Street, people laughed in her face and told her to return to her parents' home or search for a husband instead. They believed that starting a family, not a career in finance, would be where Benham would find her happily ever after (Contentworks Agency 2019).

Benham knew differently, though. She finally found a bond statistician job at Wall Street firm R.W. Pressprich & Co., and started generating precise reports about the American railroad industry despite having an unsupportive boss. As she continued working diligently, she began advancing in her company's ranks and ultimately became their top railroad analyst (Contentworks Agency 2019). Eventually, she would join the New York Stock Exchange—the first woman to do so.

Progress. The legacy she left behind showed every person doubting her ability to work on Wall Street that her intellect was not hindered by gender. In fact, it was only strengthened as her fire to prove herself grew (Contentworks Agency 2019).

Although women slowly entered the public sector in Senate, House, and governorship positions, the federal judicial branch remained unattainable until Sandra Day O'Connor. An early high-school graduate and Stanford Law attendee, O'Connor was more than qualified to hold a position as a lawyer. Unfortunately, because a scant 2 percent of law students were women in the 1950s and discriminatory attitudes still prevailed, she was forced to become a deputy county attorney in California—where she started her career working for no salary and shared an office with a secretary (Oyez n.d.).

In 1965, O'Connor decided to join local politics in Arizona, becoming an assistant attorney general and eventually winning a state senate seat in 1972, later even being elected as the Republican majority leader. After gaining a strong background in politics, she decided to become a judge and gained a position in the Maricopa County Superior Court, then later a position in the Arizona Court of Appeals. She founded the National Association of Women Judges shortly after to encourage other women that they, too, could be judges. What her career in Arizona demonstrated was important for women everywhere—because if only men evaluated the court cases and an entire half of the population was missing from the courtroom panel, then the probability of justice being rightfully served was slim (Oyez n.d.).

Because women had gained the right to vote decades earlier, appealing politically to men alone became inadequate. Now candidates also needed support from female voters. As a last plea in Ronald Reagan's presidential campaign, he promised that if he received this support from women and was elected, he would appoint the very first woman to the US Supreme Court. Then, when he successfully secured his presidential nomination and entered office, he upheld his side of the bargain and nominated Sandra Day O' Connor, who at this point had both strong legal and state court experience.

The Senate unanimously accepted her, and O'Connor became the very first female justice in 191 years of the Supreme Court's existence in the United States (Oyez n.d.). She was deeply honored to finally have the opportunity to showcase her knowledge and power, and for the next twenty-five years would serve as Supreme Court Associate Justice. In 2004, at a commencement speech back her at alma mater, she said, "Ronald Reagan knew his decision wasn't about Sandra Day O'Connor; it was about women everywhere. It was about a nation that was on its way to bridging a chasm between genders that had divided us for too long" (Sandra Day O'Connor Institute for American Democracy n.d.).

At the same time, women weren't just fighting for equal opportunities on Earth—but in space as well. In areas without gravity, gender inequality still lingered (Anderson 2018). At the very beginning of the 1960s, NASA decided to conduct a series of tests evaluating whether women had the skill and physical ability to be successful astronauts. Just as women felt discrimination in an office workplace, they felt that same discrimination in the space program: NASA shut down the Woman in Space program in 1962 despite *every woman* passing the very same tests as the NASA astronauts. Other astronauts agreed with NASA. In congressional hearings on how feasible it would be to have women go into space, John Glenn and Scott Carpenter voiced their concerns that women were unqualified because "they were not military test pilots" even though it was forbidden for women to even hold those positions (Blakemore 2020).

By 1978, when Sally Ride introduced herself to the world of space exploration, NASA no longer required astronauts to previously have been military test pilots. That said, stigma against women was still prevalent. But Ride did not allow that to deter her from applying to NASA, and she was selected out of 8,000 other people as one of only six women to be a part of the class of thirty-five. After five years of fastidious but behind-the-scenes work—from helping other astronauts on their missions to engineering a robotics arm for the International Space Station—Ride was finally granted her own mission. She would be a crew member for STS-7, a Challenger shuttle (Blakemore 2020).

As Ride was the first American woman to ever fly in space, this mission was unprecedented, unexplored territory for the media and NASA—especially ironic considering the latter had traversed planets beyond Earth.

In the mission's leadup, Ride was asked if going up would possibly prevent her from becoming pregnant in the future.

On top of that, NASA told Ride she should take a hundred tampons for the trip and even designed a makeup kit for her—that she left behind (Blakemore 2020). She was disappointed that everyone was so focused on her being a woman and said in an interview with Gloria Steinem, a political leader, "Everybody wanted to know what kind of makeup I was taking up. They didn't care about how well-prepared I was to operate the arm or deploy communication satellites" (Blakemore 2020). Eventually, she started her own organization, Sally Ride Science, which served to promote STEM careers and provide mentors for girls and women.

Ride may have been the first American woman to leave Earth, but Dorothy Vaughan, an African-American mathematician, brought with her a spirit to do more than observe aeronautical research data at NASA, specifically becoming a supervisor in its West Computers group. Because she was Black, she was separated from the other white women in both work and recreational areas. Still, she found herself interceding on behalf of her white female workers when they deserved promotions or pay raises but were not receiving recognition. In fact, engineers routinely sought Vaughan's opinion of who the best girls for any given project would be (Shetterly 2017).

Progress. As NASA's first Black supervisor, she left an imprint on history and built the future with her mentorship of others in West Computers such as Mary Jackson and Katherine Johnson (Shetterly 2017). Despite being treated even worse than her white counterparts, Vaughan fought for equality and acceptance for all women at work.

Ruth Bader Ginsburg once said, "As society sees what women can do, as women see what women can do, there will be more women out there doing things, and we'll all be better off for it"(BBC News 2020). The key word here is "we'll all"—because Ginsburg believed gender equality was not only necessary for women's freedoms but for men's as well. In 1972, she cofounded the ACLU Women's Rights Project with Brenda Feigen. Later, in the 2000s, WRP was a leading fighter in the battle to get employers to disband standardized policies assigning women as primary care-givers, instead ensuring men and women received equal benefits like parental leave. Ginsburg believed when men were constantly working, they missed the opportunity to raise their children and leave a monumental mark on their lives (Tabacco Mar 2020).

Her own experiences with gender inequality, though, were reflected strongly on the court. In the past, Ginsburg had to hide her pregnancy as a public school teacher because "schools didn't want little children to think their teacher had swallowed a watermelon" (University of California Press n.d.). The maternity leave she was then asked to take was unpaid and did not guarantee job security upon return. At the time, the Supreme Court did not see discrimination based on pregnancy as equivalent to discrimination based on sex.

Progress. After insistent fighting and attempts to broaden the perspectives of Supreme Court justices, Congress amended Title VII to state: "Discrimination on the basis of pregnancy is discrimination on the basis of sex" (University of California Press n.d.).

After researching these historical heroes, I now realize I know so little about the monumental women of the past—and I can't help but wonder how many others have made substantial changes to our society that I don't yet know about. Before researching, I never considered how in the 1800s—when the only form of transportation was horse-drawn carriages—there were no virtual reality glasses women could put on to escape their household lives. Nevertheless, all these historical heroes made progress across a multitude of sectors and changed the game for generations of women to follow. Because even as they were fighting for themselves, they blazed a trail for the women who came after.

When reading about these incredible women, I was especially inspired by Dr. Bernice Sandler, who dreamed of changing the world since she was a little girl and ended up transforming the universe for working women. Instead of allowing those who believed she came on too strong to dictate her self-worth, she used her strength to push forward. People like her make a difference in our society every day. Their choices to keep going—to shoulder past the pain and inequality—are the reason why we are able to continue breaking barriers instead of trying to repair old ones. Her strength, once ridiculed, is one reason other women can now feel strength and celebrate their perseverance.

Before this, I never realized there was a time when women had no access to credit and could only do so through their husbands (El Issa 2020). I cannot imagine how restricted they must have felt financially—unable to make their own purchases solely because of gender. Similarly, and even though I went through a phrase in middle school where I was obsessed with the idea of becoming an astronaut, I did not know NASA had created and then canceled the Women in Space program despite successful performance (Blakemore 2020).

Women in our past dedicated so much energy to moving these obstacles and are integral parts of our history that I simply took for granted before. Sometimes, I wish more of our generation could learn about these women so we realize the number of opportunities available to us now that were non-existent before.

Reading the stories of these historical heroes excites me. Their accomplishments and words of wisdom will remind future generations there was a time when extreme workplace discrimination existed in every single industry—but they persevered and showed others how to keep fighting.

Who knows? The figures in the following chapters may be showcased in the historical accounts of the future.

Chapter 3

I wonder how many dreams have been crushed by silence, even by my own. It truly saddens me how girls can love something with all their heart, but because of a lack of support from other people, they are forced to leave it behind when they grow up.

When I was in sixth grade, I was convinced I would be the world's next big singer. I distinctly remember sitting in my English class with my laptop propped open, researching the audition process for *America's Got Talent*. I had the soundtrack to "Shake It Off" already saved on my hard drive, and every day after school, while my mom went to pick up my sister and my dad was at work, I would belt out the chorus in the shower.

Was I good? Absolutely not. My voice was uneven with scratchy high pitches, and I sounded like I was gasping for breath only four seconds into the song.

One time, I was belting out another Taylor Swift song in the shower and didn't realize my sister had entered the house. At first all I could hear was the running water, but then I heard my sister's screams and quickly turned off the water.

"What happened?" I began to panic, heart racing.

Then I heard her yell loudly back from the other room, "With the sounds that were coming from the bathroom, I thought there was a dying frog in the tub." My heartrate immediately slowed, and I dejectedly turned the shower back on.

Another time during art class, while I dabbed burgundy paint onto my canvas, I began singing at a moderately loud volume. I am not joking when I say that after a solid four minutes, the three unfortunate souls who had been sitting at my table left to sit somewhere else. And not to mention the chorus teacher who patted my shoulder and told me there were plenty other things I was good at after he had heard me audition…

I think the funniest part is that I simply did not care. I thought it was a message I was on the right track.

Except pursuing this dream became harder to do as the days went on. I could not find a single person supportive of my endeavors—except for *The Voice* judges on my Xbox who, as long as I sang the right words, said I was sensational and an icon!

But characters in a simulation can only sustain someone's dreams for so long, so one day, I woke up and just stopped.

I stopped participating in karaoke, stopped screeching out lyrics in my friends' cars when my favorite music came on, and stopped humming along to heartbreakingly beautiful melodies. I stopped singing in the shower too.

Isn't it crazy how a dream that consumed a child's life for so long can disappear just like that?

In our society, where money regulates the opportunities people have access to, the reality that a woman can complete the same tasks with identical educational credentials and still be compensated less than a man is terrifying.

As students, we are often told if we study hard and learn the material, our grades will reflect that. When our teachers mark our math tests, they don't sit down and immediately give a 5 percent bonus to all the boys. They would lose their jobs and perhaps never be able to teach again for showing such blatant bias.

Yet if high school is supposed to prepare us for the real world, and I never received a 95 percent to a boy's 100 percent, why, when I join the workforce, will I potentially receive ninety-five cents to a man's dollar? Why was I given a level playing field in school if the moment I step into the workforce, I could run around the bases six times and still never score a run? We will never know at what precise point the rules of the game change, and I suppose that is part of the fun—to guess when the playbook will be switched out with cheat codes.

I always went through life thinking that in times of loneliness and strife, most give up. It never really occurred to me there are people who instead take advantage of these situations to enact positive change. So after reading and interviewing women who were discriminated against in pay, I was pleasantly surprised. Every single one of them chose to persevere—even as almost everyone abandoned their side. They continued to fight, which meant risking others leaving too.

Hearing their stories made me think of my own situation. I had been looking at everything through such a negative lens. I constantly blamed other people for my decision to stop singing, but at no point did anyone actually tell me to stop. No one took my voice away. I chose to be quiet. I could have searched for people who believed in me. I could have continued to practice so I could become better and prove everyone who thought otherwise wrong. But I didn't. It would have been amazing to have more support, but we can only succeed if we are ready to support ourselves.

Who knows where I would have gone if I hadn't let the silence get the best of me?

But the world is much bigger than what I wanted to do. There were so many moments I have laughed at other's ambitions too. Like the time my friend told me she wanted to become a fashion designer and came to school in a mismatched ensemble with a sock as a headband. And when my sister was convinced she would go to law school and become the next president when she could barely spell the word "intelligent." Instead of laughing, I could have supported them in achieving their dreams.

After all, we can only be the next superstar if *we* believe we can. And we have to support the people we love.

Chapter 4

I did not learn what the figure-eight shaped infinity symbol meant in the *domain and range of quadratic functions* lecture in math class but rather afterward, when I spent six continuous hours letting helpless parabola-shaped drops slip from my eyes the night before a major exam.

My dad found me sobbing at my desk with a paper torn in half from my pen scribbling, mumbling repeatedly, "My pain over math is infinite."

I could not graph it so someone else could find the domain and range.

I cannot even begin to count the number of times I have cried over a math problem like this—both in my room and in public. One time, during a calculus test, after attempting each question and failing miserably to find a single correct answer, I had to leave the room before I let out a flood of waterworks in front of everyone. When I came back, my eyesight was so blurry I could barely read my own handwriting. Every number looked the same. Even now, I regularly find myself blindly copying down whatever my math teacher is saying on a piece of paper and then double-checking my schedule to make sure I have not deliriously walked into French class instead.

I admit math has given me much heartbreak over the years. Yet, strange as it sounds, I love it unconditionally.

Growing up, I spent long afternoons sitting in my mother's lap while she guided my stubby pencil across a blank page, whispering numbers in my ear as I wrote them down. Every number I put into a formula, every variable I isolate, has a remnant of my mother pressed into it, and I know even when I am at college, a part of her will always live in my math notebook.

And so despite the suffering math has put me through, my life is empty without it, and I would not know what to do if I couldn't depend on the constant of crying over domain and range.

I once experienced that hollowness during a conversation with my dad's acquaintance at a party when he asked me what my favorite subject was. When I answered "math," his face, previously curious, contorted into a flabbergasted expression as if the thought of someone deriving pleasure from solving equations physically hurt his brain.

He then laughed a little, clapped my parents on the back, and guffawed, "You got an ambitious one there. Thought she would be interested in something more girly." My heart dropped. I smiled sheepishly, a little ashamed and embarrassed.

In a way, it makes sense.

Perhaps when he saw me—a small, young girl who occasionally wore Justice leggings because everything else was in the washing machine—he couldn't envision me willingly holding a graphing calculator and computing the slope of curves.

Few female friends of mine will say their favorite class is math. I am sure a big factor is the subject's level of difficulty. But a part of me feels we are conditioned to feel it is okay to not like it because we don't *need* to like it.

When we think of mathematicians or math teachers, our minds leap to men in suits with a textbook clutched under their arms. We women are merely their students. It saddens me not everyone has had someone in their lives to teach them math is a subject worthy of being their favorite.

One afternoon, I was researching at the library when I came across the story of Aileen Rizo, a Latino woman whose dream as a little girl was a job in math education. After hearing so many girls around her say they hated math, she hoped she could encourage them to pursue the subject.

This was *exactly* the type of woman I was looking for. I was excited to read further, eagerly anticipating success stories of all the girls' lives she changed. Instead, I saw a picture of her with a group of young girls, holding up papers that did not have math problems—but the words, "Equal work deserves equal pay."

Growing up, Aileen Rizo found herself to be the minority in many situations.

In her calculus class in high school, she was the sole Latina. Out of her entire family, she was the first to pursue post-secondary education and receive a college degree despite growing up in an impoverished South Phoenix neighborhood.

When she acquired a position at the Fresno County Office of Education in California as a math consultant who helped other teachers become familiar with different methods of training students, she was the lone woman who worked full-time in the mathematics department (CSUSB 2019).

As an Indian girl, I am used to being in the minority. And since sixth grade, I have also been the youngest in my math classes—two years younger and several inches shorter than my classmates. As a sophomore in high school, my math class was entirely boys with the exception of two girls. I have had a male math teacher for as long as I can remember.

As I read Rizo's background, though, I was thrilled to see she not only followed her own dream—she became an inspiration for others to share that dream too.

During the summer of 2012, Aileen Rizo had finished a lunch meeting with her coworkers and was depositing a bundle of papers and laptop into her work bag, wiping away strands of her hair that were stuck to her face, when three of her male colleagues began to loudly discuss their salaries.

She turned away to allow them to engage in this discussion without her presence.

But then Rizo overheard the newest hire, someone she herself had welcomed into the company, say, "I just signed my contract, and I got Step 9" [roughly $79,100] (Hutchins n.d.).

Rizo flinched, then froze as the other men in the room began to clap him on the back and express their loud congratulations.

Her head began spinning. She stumbled light-headed as she tried to convince herself she had heard incorrectly, that the loud cheers in the background were because they wrapped up a successful meeting. Blinking back tears, Rizo walked angrily out of the room (Hutchins n.d.).

This man had walked into the company barely a week ago. He did not have a degree in math. Still, he was almost at the top of the pay scale, while she was still on Step 1, which was $17,000 less. She was appalled and horrified.

With two master's degrees and thirteen years of math teaching experience, Rizo was one of the most qualified in her department.

At the Fresno County Office of Education, employees were compensated on a ten-step pay scale—Step 1 being the lowest level of compensation and Step 10 the highest. Three years prior, Rizo moved, uprooting her entire family from Arizona to California where she had spent the last thirty-six months working exceptionally hard.

At this institution, employees' starting salaries were based on their previous salaries plus 5 percent, which was the way things had always been. Rizo felt her heart break because many women receive lower pay at previous workplaces if they had been out of the office to give birth to and raise their children. Her new, highly-paid male coworker had experienced no such setbacks.

According to the Center for American Progress, another such pay inequity is when women work in a "women-dominated occupation." In this case, they are compensated less since the job is labelled "women's work." In decade after decade of pay disparity, if a woman was not being compensated fairly at her workplace and chose to leave, instead of being given a fair amount of pay at her new workplace, the pay gap perpetuates her position there too (Bleiweis 2021).

As the breadwinner in her family, Rizo is responsible for taking care of her daughters—and that $17,000 could have been used to support her kids' emotional and physical well-being and provide them the best childhood possible (AAUW 2020).

Unfortunately, Rizo is not the only woman who has experienced the pay gap. In the United States, during this time, women made an average of eighty cents to a man's dollar (Depaulo 2018).

Their paychecks—the measure of how much they are worth to their companies—have been a constant reminder their efforts were not appreciated and are of less value. I can't even begin to imagine how demoralizing it must have been to continue coming to work each day, doing the same job as the man sitting nearby, and leaving with hundreds of dollars less in their bank accounts.

Many women still might not even know the Equal Pay of 1963 exists, which makes it illegal for employers to give men a higher wage than a woman for the same amount of work (Depaulo 2018).

Rizo expressed she "did not know her rights" either, but she could sense something was wrong (Depaulo 2018). However, a part of Rizo wanted to simply accept the inequality as-is, as do many other women who have a fear of recrimination.

According to gender equality director Kathryn Nawrockyi, "People don't report these incidents, either because they accept such behavior as the norm in their organization or because they are afraid of losing their job in cases such as pay discrimination or sexual harassment" (Minter 2016).

Rizo continually analyzed the repercussions of what might happen if she raised this issue. Would she lose her job? What if she could no longer provide for her family? When she entered her house later that day, dejected and sorrowful, her daughters came sprinting into her arms.

As she welcomed them into a hug, feeling serene for the first time since that dreadful lunch meeting, she mumbled to herself, "What I choose to do—or not to do—will impact my girls. I want them to grow up in a world where they are treated equally" (Depaulo 2018.).

Rizo confronted many people in her workplace but was met with great opposition.

Her protests of, "You have to pay a man and woman the same for the same amount of work—that is the *law*," were silenced by both the human resources department and her supervisor. Rizo was heartbroken. The love and passion she had for her workplace was crumbling, especially now that the very people who were supposed to listen had cast aside everything she had done for them and refused to even hear her out.

It was clear everyone wanted her to accept the situation and move on. But a deep sense of responsibility was pulsing in her body, even stronger than the blood rushing through her veins.

She reminded herself, "Whatever a woman decides in the workplace, she decides not only for herself, but for those who come after" (CSUSB 2019).

If she did nothing, other women would eventually find themselves in her shoes and be met with even more resistance and hurt. Even if she could shoulder through the pain of being compensated unequally, she refused to let the next woman suffer too.

She decided if speaking up at her company was not enough, she would find a lawyer and take the matter to court.

In 2014, Rizo put her case forward in the US District Court for the Eastern District of California, under the 1963 federal Equal Pay Act, on the grounds the salary of a new employee should not be calculated based on pay received before in a different company.

Rizo faced a crushing defeat.

The three judges overseeing the case posited that the Equal Pay Act ensured an employer could not base compensation decisions on gender. However, in this case, the factor was previous salaries. Therefore, they concluded, Rizo's employer had not infringed on the Equal Pay Act.

This ruling against Rizo exemplifies the necessity to pass federal legislation that completely erases employers' ability to calculate current salary based on past compensation. The Paycheck Fairness Act, which was introduced to Congress but has not passed due to political opposition, would strengthen the strictness of the "factor other than sex" part of the Equal Pay clause. Employers would have to provide a "business justification" as to why the pay between men and women is different (Hutchins n.d.).

The court's decision nearly broke her. Throughout the process, Rizo continually wrestled with guilt and misery, because while she was filing a deposition and fighting for equal pay, her girls were at home without their mother.

I cannot imagine Rizo's struggle between which was more important—her daughters or fighting for justice.

Even though Rizo was ready to admit defeat and give up, her husband pushed her to keep going. She became a regular at the American Association of University Women meetings and eventually became part of the organization, learning to love sharing her story instead of hiding it.

Eventually, on December 11, 2017, Rizo walked into the courtroom again. This time, all of the judges on the en banc court ruled in Rizo's favor.

One of them, Judge Stephen Reinhardt, wrote in his ruling, "Women are told they are not worth as much as men. Allowing prior salary to justify a wage differential perpetuates this message, entrenching in salary systems an obvious means of discrimination" (Hutchins n.d.). Rizo felt she had finally accomplished her goal—the one she had been working diligently on since that fateful post-lunch meeting conversation.

Unfortunately, this same official, Judge Reinhardt, died before the decision was "officially filed," and the Supreme Court deemed it invalid. Chief Justice Roberts expressed, "Judges are appointed for life, but not for eternity" (Hutchins n.d.).

The Supreme Court denied Rizo's request to hear the case again.

However, her journey was not over. Aileen Rizo spread her story to locals in her community. In 2018, she ran for the California State Assembly to represent the twenty-third district, successfully receiving the Democratic Primary nomination but unfortunately losing to the incumbent Republican.

When asked why she ran, she answered, "He vetoed all the equal pay legislation for which I testified" (Hutchins n.d.).

Today, Rizo is the associate director of the AIMS Center for Math and Science Education, still teaching and designing new methods of math and science to gifted students and minorities who lack the opportunity to explore STEM fields.

She also still coaches teachers, hoping their high school students will look at her and say, "I look just like her and she's my teacher's math teacher!" (Hutchins n.d.)

My research on Rizo concluded with this profound quote from her: "I don't want another girl to feel after she's worked so hard that she's not worth the same as the man sitting next to her" (PowHer NY 2014).

I have shed thousands of tears and devoted many hours of hard work to math. Thanks to Rizo staying strong and her contributions through her journey for equal pay, those tears and dedication can mean something.

This story was not, initially, what I set out to read. I sat there with a pencil poised in my hand, but I struggled to put words down on paper. I wondered what I would have done in her shoes.

Would I have convinced myself to forget what I heard, then saddling myself with guilt for not saying anything? Would I have chosen to persevere after almost everyone abandoned me and risked the rest leaving too? And would I have admitted defeat after the judges ruled against me in my first attempt?

It is no secret we live in a world where the wealthiest are the most successful. If women cannot afford certain necessities, how can they possibly pursue a higher education and gain the skills they need to thrive in the workplace? If they want to save up for a seaside ranch or even just set aside money for medical emergencies—it will take significantly longer.

And the pay gap does not just persist when they are working—it carries to retirement, always ensuring their opportunities are limited. Do short-term goals even exist in their vocabulary then if everything they want will take forever to fulfill? Why am I learning about inflation in economics class if the dollar women receive was always going to be less than the man's anyway?

I realize now the resilience Aileen Rizo showed was infinite: Time after time, defeat after defeat, she persevered and rose up.

People like Rizo give me hope for not only other women but for myself. I wish I could tell all the people in this world who think math is too masculine a subject for girls to evaluate just how wrong they are. And the next time someone makes a face at my answer, I will not smile sheepishly. I will grin proudly because I refuse to feel shame for liking a subject my mother showed me how to love.

Chapter 5

I could write page after page about the injustice many women have had to face—but Taylor Swift says it best with her three-minute song, "The Man."

For years, as a dedicated Swiftie, I have fended off comments insulting Taylor Swift's craft, the soundtrack to my everyday life. I was always in awe of her song-writing abilities; the way she made the most traumatic moments a poetic experience for everyone listening. There is not a single song she has produced I do not want to stand on a chair and scream into empty air. I even have a running page of some of her lyrics I hold close to my heart starred in my Google drive.

One day when I sat down to write, "The Man" started playing. In that moment, I discovered the difference between listening to a song and *listening* to a song. For so long, I had just nodded my head to the catchy beat, swaying my shoulders in time to its steady cadence. But now, instead of wanting to bounce, a deep pit of anger formed in my chest. My hands, which used to drum rhythms on the glass of my worktable, were now clenched so tightly I could see white nail-shaped imprints on my palms. I do not know how, for two years, I could have just ignored the powerful lyrics she had woven and *danced* instead. It felt like I had disgraced her craft.

Now I begin each writing session with "The Man." I imagine a chorus of the women profiled in my book belting it out with their loudest voices. Much of their self-regard and assurance of their abilities came from their workplace—after all, they gave so much of their time and energy to their careers. But what about when they become mothers?

It isn't only the pay gap that hurts women. I cannot even keep track of the number of conversations I have had with people equating gender inequality to just "women are paid less than men." We don't realize there is so much more to the issue that because we are too focused on the numbers.

According to political news from WHYY, the US is the only "advanced economy" that does not have mandated paid maternity leave (Kurtzleben 2015). In 1993, the Family Medical Leave Act passed and allotted up to twelve weeks of *unpaid* leave to care for family members, such as a new-born baby. Unfortunately, this rule only applies to workers at companies with over fifty employees, and they need to have worked there for at least a year (US Department of Labor 2023). After nine months of pregnancy and then childbirth, too many mothers must return to the workforce and now have to juggle their jobs *and* a baby on little sleep instead of retreating to the comfort of their homes for rest and healing. Of course, if their work is not of absolute high quality, their jobs are still in jeopardy. With a new mouth to feed at home, it becomes a situation of literally life or death.

The US also does not require companies to offer childcare benefits. In 2022, a survey showed many families expected to pay upwards of $10,000 for child care that year—for many an incredible and impossible to pay amount (Gabrielle 2022). And according to another survey conducted by the Center for American Progress, when financial situations arise, mothers are 40 percent more likely to take on childcare issues than fathers (Schochet 2019). Essentially, these women must put childcare issues before their career goals because they are the ones traditionally expected to take on the role of caregiver when straits get dire.

I was given the privilege of talking to Reema, Jenny Tale, Olivia Thomas, and Amelia Weller to discuss how workplaces are designed for men, not women. In the following chapters, I will explore the disadvantages women face and what society needs to keep in mind to combat these situations. After all, playing a rigged game means fewer victories.

Chapter 6

When I was in third grade, my family decided—after a warm pasta bowl, soup drowning in cheddar flakes, and perfectly drizzled vinegar salad at Olive Garden—it would be an amazing idea to make a stop at our local movie theater to watch an Indian movie some friends had been raving about.

I was less than thrilled about it, but my sister and I didn't really have a choice, so we walked solemnly past the bright *Minions* poster and into a different auditorium. If I had known the characters would be covered in blood—the same color as the tomato sauce coating my ravioli lunch just a few hours ago—I would have put up more of a fight.

The movie consisted of betrayal, death, and unfortunately for me, lots of blood. I spent two out of the three hours with my palms covering my eyes and the other hour motioning my dad to tell me if anything looked suspiciously scary so I could proceed to close my eyes.

I trembled in my seat. Something about two men fighting each other with a sword then having the life force seep out of their veins I could not stomach. I remember telling my mom when they were carted to the emergency room as the hero's blood spewed from his chest that if she didn't want to see the leftovers of Olive Garden on the floor of our local Regal Movie Theater, it would be best to leave early.

Unfortunately, I seemed to be the only one terrified. Even my sister, five years old, had her wide eyes glued to the screen. In fact, every time I let out a muffled scream in genuine desperation, she looked at me weirdly and said, "You know the blood is fake, right? It's just makeup." I couldn't believe it. The same girl who shrieked every time I turned off the lights was somehow watching a person now having their leg cut off with no problem.

As I left the movie theater that day, another realization startled me: While maybe sword fights are not common now, there are still people like ER nurses and surgeons who see people regularly covered in *real* blood, and instead of running away screaming, they save them. Their entire days and sometimes nights are dedicated to easing the pain of others and ensuring their heart beats on for at least one more day. But me? For the next six nights, I did not sleep.

Every time I closed my eyes, I just saw two men with blood-covered faces, and I tossed and turned, trying to run away from them but failing. On particularly sleepless nights, I would resort to crawling into my parents' bedroom and curling up next to my dad. Yet I constantly grappled with the idea that while I was having nightmares about death, doctors were out there keeping people alive.

Seven years later and I am still terrified by blood. I refuse to watch any movie with my parents, fearing the main characters may start wailing on each other and I would have to bear the consequence of seeing them splattered in blood.

I had the good fortune to meet my next interviewee, Reema, in person. I was very excited to come face-to-face with one of the people I admire for their ability to see not the horror in blood, but rather its vitality in keeping us flush with life.

I asked my standard first interview question: "What was your dream as a little girl?"

She smiled and said softly, "When I was younger and lived in India, I dreamed of becoming a surgeon."

I tilted my head slightly. "Why? Weren't you scared of the pain and the blood?"

Reema paused to think. "No. I never once thought it was scary because I did not let my mind wander to the idea that by performing an operation on someone, I would be inflicting pain on them. I instead saw myself taking away that pain from other people."

Reema remembers visiting her grandfather in a hospital, where she knew the doctor very well, as a sophomore in high school. He invited her into the surgery room while her grandfather was sleeping, pointing out the large, brass metal instruments but cautioning her not to touch them—though she was tempted to run her fingers across their smooth surfaces. She squinted her eyes in awe as she turned her face upward to gaze at the room's beaming lights. As she stood there next to the surgeon, she could not help but feel a warm rush of gratitude for his expertise and ability to improve her grandfather's condition—a feat few could accomplish.

Reema realized there was an unspoken trust between a patient's family and the doctor because their life is quite literally in the hands of the surgeon. She realized she wished to build that connection with someone one day and save a person's life. As she grew up, she spent every moment she could at the hospital. Underlying that dream was striving to become independent, go to work every day, and bring home a paycheck that was completely hers.

Reema reminisced, explaining, "People knew me by two things: my radiant smile they fondly described as 'sweet as honey' and my passion for learning. I loved to explore new subjects no matter the difficulty level or aptitude required. In fact, I loved the classes I had the most difficulty excelling in because it reminded me that life is more than just demonstrating to other people we know something but proving to ourselves we learned something."

I nodded in agreement. "Many people forget to partake in the joy of learning. They mechanically study because they want good grades on tests or a job that pays well. They don't enjoy the process."

Reema did, though. She woke up at the early hours of dawn to do her homework with a quietly flickering candle resting by her wooden desk, then did all the household tasks. After that, she would bike to school, bike back, clean the entire house until there was not a single spot left, and retreat to her desk where she would study until late in the evening.

Her mother couldn't speak English, her father was constantly out of the house on work trips, and she had no older siblings or cousins to teach her. She took on the responsibility of learning herself, then in her free time passed that knowledge on to her younger, much rowdier brothers. No one really understood why she worked so hard. After all, her grandmother had left school in fifth grade and her mother stopped her education at eighth grade.

Reema paused in her storytelling and looked me in the eye to say, "I wanted to become something. I wanted to be known for more than just being the girl who smiled beautifully and worked diligently." She knew that with her passion for learning and her dedication to hard work she could reach unimaginable heights—and bring her family there too.

In 1998, she married her husband, an employee at a small sales company. Unfortunately, they were not able to settle straight into a comfortable lifestyle in India, as her husband received word that he must travel overseas to America to carry out his work. He had already worked in various states across the US for the past two years, but this time—ten days into their marriage—he would bring Reema, a small-town girl, with him.

Reema had never stepped foot outside of India, unless she counted moments spent tracing continents in her geography textbook. Traveling to America was not even a thought she had dared entertain. At this point, she was halfway through her full-ride scholarship masters, but she dropped out of the program to support her husband in his ambitions.

"I believed America was the land of dreams and opportunities," Reema said. "We grew up hearing that was where people ventured off in search of fulfilling their wishes."

She was excited to take part in this journey. For the first time in her life, she let herself dream a little bigger.

Reema and her husband moved temporarily into a one-bedroom apartment. From the day they settled in Minnesota, her husband resumed his long workdays: seven in the morning to nine at night.

Reema decided that she, too, would search for a job, but discovered she needed a résumé to be considered for any position. A résumé? Reema had no idea how to build a résumé, especially when she had no experience—just a half-finished degree from a college in India, which American companies would never recognize. She couldn't and wouldn't lie. And their financial situation was too tight for her to find a way to add to or finish her education.

Although Reema could have volunteered or tried to gain experience through other means, she was afraid it would not be enough. After all, according to a *Forbes* article based on an internal Hewlett Packard report, "Men apply for a job when they meet only 60 percent of the qualifications, but women apply only if they meet 100 percent of them." The HP report also states that 22 percent of women expressed their primary reason for not applying for a certain job was, "I didn't think they would hire me since I didn't meet the qualifications, and I didn't want to put myself out there if I was likely to fail" (Mohr 2014).

That first one-bedroom apartment was not temporary. In fact, it was Reema's holding cell from 1998 to 2003. Because of her lack of experience and work permit, she was unable to seek employment. For the fourteen hours her husband was at work each day, Reema searched for fulfillment alone, now describing those five years as the "worst time of [her] life because there was no end to the waiting period."

I put my pencil down. "What did you do when your husband was gone?"

Reema answered thoughtfully, "While I was in my twenties, everyone else in the apartment complex were senior citizens who barely left the house, and I struggled to make a single friend. I didn't know how to drive, and even if I did we only had one car, which my husband needed for work. Our residential complex was isolated and in the middle of nowhere—it was too difficult for me to walk anywhere, and there was no public transportation available to take me to a library."

During the summers she was able to jog outside at least, but in the freezing Minnesota winters the only sunlight she saw were tiny beams flooding her room through the crevices of her two windows.

Because she and her husband were filing for green cards so he could continue working in America, she could not go back to India to see her parents. And even if she was allowed, they wouldn't have even been able to afford a round trip flight. During the beginning of the twenty-first century, calling people overseas was a privilege—each minute cost fifty-five cents—and they weren't able to purchase their own phone until 2002. Reema, who had rarely gone a single day without seeing her mom, was having difficulty picturing her mother and missed hearing the sound of her voice.

Only one thing gave her company—her deep passion for learning.

"Slowly, I filled my apartment with SAT chemistry subject tests, math booklets, and manuals on how to perform basic computer functions. I kept my mind sharp and busy, determined that I would not lose the knowledge I had spent my childhood committing to memory," she described.

In 2003, they moved out of the apartment to their own home. Reema felt her hopes rise slightly, thinking that after enduring five years of absolute horror, she would be able to perhaps finally go back to school and finish her education.

Then, shortly after moving into the new house, she found out she was pregnant.

Reema was ecstatic to bring her daughter into the world, as her daughter would be the companion she so desperately sought. As she recovered from childbirth, she sat with her computer on her lap to take free online courses in chemistry while her baby slept peacefully next to her. However, she knew her dreams of working would never be fulfilled.

For one, where would her child go? She couldn't leave a seven-month old baby in a home by herself, and they still did not have enough money to pay for daycare. Even if they somehow did scavenge the funds, everything she earned at work would just go to the childcare center. She didn't see the point of being disconnected from her daughter and never seeing her because of a job. During 2021, the US Treasury Department published data showing the average US family with at least one child under the age of five will find themselves spending 13 percent of their income on childcare (Taketa 2023).

But over time Reema's self-esteem was eroding away. As her daughter made friends, she too slowly built connections with their moms, who were fortunately all financially stable enough to work and provide their children paid care.

"I would always avert my eyes when they began talking about how much work they have to do or how uncomfortable their work attire was." Reema shrugged her shoulders. "I mean, for a while, I felt inferior. They were making a difference in their workplace while I was changing diapers and wiping baby formula off my clothes. I wanted to go to meetings, talk to different people… explore the world."

Reema took a sip of her water. "But I also realized that many of my friends who were working were not as happy as I thought they were."

Research supports this. Zaira Reynoso, a mother to a newborn infant and another girl, chose to work from home after seeing that her family would have to pay $1,500 a month for childcare (Taketa 2023). Throughout this balancing act, she spent nights crying in bed next to her daughter because she felt she was "failing at both her job and being a good mom" (Taketa 2023). Reynoso constantly felt ashamed and guilty for not being able to provide the kids she loved more than anything with the care she wished she could give—while also juggling her job and attempting to give 100 percent to her workplace.

I asked Reema, "How long did you feel this sadness about your life?"

"As my eldest daughter grew and I welcomed my second child into the family, I found myself feeling happier. I looked forward to the evenings spent by the kitchen table, helping them with their math homework problems, or reading over their English essays," she replied affectionately.

From a young age, she taught her daughters that no matter how hard people tried, they could never take away their knowledge. Her children grew up in a loving household with everything they ever wanted given to them. Reema made sure of that. She sacrificed buying jewelry and nice clothes to ensure her girls had all the books they wanted, art classes at their disposal, sports lessons to go to, and limited-edition school supplies.

The one thing, though, that she expected in return was their hard work. She said that unimaginable doors are opened and dreams are fulfilled—as long as we try our best in everything we approach and do. Success only comes with diligence.

One day, as she sat down to drink a cup of tea, her eldest daughter looked up from her history notes and inquired curiously, "If our dreams come true when we work hard, why didn't yours?" To say Reema was shocked to hear that come from an eleven-year-old child was an understatement.

She didn't answer right away. It took her a couple of days to think of a response. And that's when it hit her.

"My dream to become something had transformed into something else. I now dreamed my daughters could do everything I had not been able to do and more." Reema looked at me with wide eyes. "For so long, I thought all my hard work as a child was wasted. That by working more, I would have been able to gain more knowledge. But when I realized my dreams had changed without me even knowing it, I knew the knowledge I possess allows me to understand more. I can use it to help other people, not just myself."

But that still doesn't mean that, because of her gender, she hadn't missed out on several opportunities to grow and expand outside of home life. She believes strongly that if a woman has lost years in the workplace, she should be deemed eligible for programs that help redevelop her career and provide her with learning opportunities and coaching to reach that stage again.

She understood childcare was so expensive in part because of liability insurance and the large number of employers required to run a successful facility (Slyter 2021). But the societal expectations that women are primary caretakers and should be the ones to sacrifice employment or educational opportunities demands attention. If national childcare remains costly and only offered at some companies, then women will forever be limited. Paying care costs for one child is already a hefty task—and with more children come more bills.

When we discussed this, Reema strongly declared, "This should become a matter of the government. They should search for more methods to reduce the cost of childcare, whether they subsidize childcare industries or look at possible legislative responses. They could also help small businesses include childcare benefits to their employees by providing financial assistance. I am by no means a qualified, experienced advisor, but I was a victim, and my experiences hold merit too."

There are other answers, though: Workplaces could allow employees to bring their children to work and provide office daycare as a company benefit. If that is not a feasible option, employers should establish flexible work hours, allowing caregivers to comfortably divide their attention between kids and work the way they want to.

This not only eliminates the cost factor but also guilt associated with leaving their children at home or in a stranger's hands. I still don't think I fully understand how if women are supposed to fulfill the traditional role of caretaker—as designated by societal standards—there are not more opportunities for them to achieve those obligations? Should childcare not be free? These women, when they go to the workplace, are working for the betterment of their company and the wider economy. If they are upset and guilty over leaving their child or abandoning them in a time where both mother and child need each other, then the company itself is hurting. We have evolved to a time when women have become a crucial force in the workplace—and we should be commemorating their potential, not hindering it.

I chewed on my pencil thoughtfully. "It seemed like for so long, you blamed yourself. Have you realized now there was a bigger factor in play?"

Reema answered, "If the expense of taking care of my first child had been voided, I perhaps would have finally received the opportunity to pursue my education. Who knows what feats I could have accomplished by today? But I also think more information on the hiring process should be published so women know what companies are really looking for instead of proceeding on incorrect expectations and realizing when it is too late."

But Reema still thinks being able to take care of her daughters and help shape them to become strong, powerful women is an incredible accomplishment in itself.

"To all the little girls who had big dreams like me," she says, "you should continue plowing through life with steady drive and ambition. Don't have a goal-oriented mindset or measure your success by how many milestones you were able to achieve. Instead, explore life. Enjoy the process of learning. It is a life-skill, something as important to know and practice as brushing your teeth."

Reema has no regrets. She may have come to America with expectations of becoming a member of the workforce, but she became a mother here, and her legacy will continue with her two daughters. No matter where she chooses to go in life, her dream will live on.

Talking to Reema about her childhood dreams of surgery did not evaporate my fear of blood. When I am flipping through the wide catalog of shows on my television, I still squeeze my eyes shut in desperation every time I see red liquid dripping down the screen, even though I recognize there are people brave enough to help the injured.

While my fear of killing and blood is familiar to me, I found myself grappling with unfamiliar emotions after our interview.

I am frustrated for Reema even if she herself has come to peace with how things happened. She did everything right—she worked hard, studied day and night, and helped her brothers and cousins also gain knowledge (though they never learned to love learning the way she did). Her class rank in high school was number two. Her peers voted her "most-likely to be successful in the future." But with no résumé and no childcare, Reema's ability to display her talents to the companies she wanted to join became moot.

How can America be the land of dreams—the place people willingly leave their homes, parents, and childhoods for—when stories like these exist?

It is because of people like Reema. Her daughters will grow up in America, carrying on the torch their mother lit with her fiery passion.

Reema might be one of the bravest and strongest people I have ever met. She wakes up every day and fulfills the role of a mother while also teaching her children how to become writers of their own stories. The obstacles she was able to overcome on her journey from India to America display her monumental resilience.

Everyone has different criteria for what they believe comprises a hero. For so long, I worshipped nurses and doctors for doing something I never could. But now, I see the hero in Reema—because she teaches her children to love learning by sharing *her* love for it, and in doing so she is building the next generation of contributing, eager leaders.

The women in my life, including the ones I have had the privilege of hearing stories from, have become an integral support system and part of my lifestyle. As these figures join the other important women already present in my life, I will look back on their stories, including Reema's, as I live out my own.

Chapter 7

I always joked that my sister might have been my mom and dad's favorite child, but I was my grandmother's favorite. From the moment I opened my eyes and unclenched my tiny fist, my grandmother saw me as not another granddaughter but rather her own daughter. I followed her around the house, lifting up the veil of her sari and going underneath the folds of her dress, then screaming in confusion because the world had suddenly gone dark. When I first learned how to roll over, it was my grandmother who excitedly grabbed my dad's phone to take pictures, even though she didn't know the difference between the camera and home button. It was her hand I grabbed onto when I took my first steps.

From day one, she has been my biggest supporter, even though I have not seen her in almost four years and her visits to America span six months at most. Thousands of miles of ocean separate us. When I go to bed she wakes up, and when I come home from school she is standing outside the front door on a different continent. She cheers me on in every journey I decide to undertake. When I told her I was writing my own book and would be a published author, she made me promise she would be the first person to purchase and read the finished work.

My grandmother believes in me when no one else does. I remember long summer nights in India when I would tell her about how scared I was for the future because I didn't think I was smart enough. After all, growing up, my teachers had told my parents that, while I showed an admirable hard-working spirit, I lagged behind my peers cognitively. It was my grandmother who told me to forge on and work hard anyway—even when other people did not think I could make it.

Listening to Reema's story reminded me how lucky I am to have a family that has supported me in every endeavor I have chosen. I have a grandmother who has taught me that no matter what the world throws at me or whoever is unsupportive, she will always love me the most.

I had the amazing privilege of interviewing three women whose workplace experiences have been far from perfect. They have faced obstacles that could have broken them and their spirit. But they chose to persevere. They came back to their workplace ready to take on more challenges, and while they sometimes found themselves at extremely low points in their self-esteem, they came out stronger. Most importantly, every one of these women decided to use those difficulties to make a difference in other women's lives. Whether it be joining organizations, writing their own books, or teaching large groups of people (including men) on workplace behavior, I was inspired to become more like them.

They also still had love. Even when they almost lost their jobs, faced dehumanizing treatment, or had their voices silenced, they still, during our interviews, cautioned me to curb my anger toward society. They showed me how even men face the repercussions of gender inequality and it is not fair to simply pin the blame on them. They also chose, instead of simply sitting in resentment, to share their stories with me so other girls could see how they can channel their anger to make a difference.

I am honored I was given the opportunity to interview and talk to them. They had no idea who I was and—as we sat down on opposite ends of a phone call—I could not help but imagine myself in their position a few years from now. It is a question I have continually grappled with as I write this book, just like I once wondered if I was smart enough to be success-ful. Do I have the courage to be resilient in my workplace? Will I use my struggles to aid others in their efforts to move up? I know with these women's voices resounding in my head, I can at least journey through life never feeling alone.

Chapter 8

In middle school, I discovered a guilty pleasure on YouTube—Dhar Mann's account. His videos made me feel less ashamed for falling into the rabbit hole of clicking on all those carefully suggested videos the algorithm pushed just for me. After all, although I was ignoring the history assignments piling up on my course dashboard, I was learning real lessons about the present world.

For two years, I eagerly devoured stories about rich girls humiliating their poor friend's Halloween costume, an evil babysitter mistreating a kid and no one believing him, and students taking a prank on their teacher too far. I kept watching them because the "bad guys" in the situation always got what they deserved, and it gave me a rush of happiness to see justice occur, even if only on a laptop screen.

When I stumbled upon "Male Boss Treats Female Employees Unfair at Work, He Lives to Regret It," I immediately clicked on it. For the first five minutes, I sat on the edge of my chair, fists clenched in barely suppressed anger, as I watched the male boss ignore his female employee's hard work then scream at her for adding her own personal touch to the designs. A bitter taste formed in my mouth watching the boss and other male employees prop their feet up on their desks while a Sunday night football rerun played lazily in the background. They dreamed of making big corporate deals as the women in the room next door actually worked to make it happen (Mann 2020). But when the female employee quit to create her own design company, I did not feel that same rush of satisfaction I usually experienced to see a happy ending.

A part of me was proud because I know we can create our own happy endings and serve retribution to those who try to deny us this privilege. Another part of me was crunching numbers, calculating how many women had encountered this very same situation without anyone knowing it because their stories weren't dramatized for millions of viewers.

One day, my dad came home from work, set his briefcase down on the ground, then wiped his ink-stained hands on his office pants. He looked at me and said he had spoken to his coworker about my book. She mentioned she had a niece, Jenny Tale, who had faced discriminatory workplace practices and was willing to share her experiences with me, anonymously. I was overjoyed but also very nervous. It was my first interview, and I had a list of potential questions pulled up on my laptop. Then I picked up my phone, and Mrs. Tale's voice filled the air.

I began, as usual, by softly asking: "What was your dream as a little girl?"

As a little girl, Mrs. Tale made commercials with Barbies she found in her parents' bedroom, dressing them in bright clothes and changing her voice to match the tone of the characters in her advertisement. On starry nights, she would whimsically stare out her window, thinking of working in a city where she could wear a suit to her office every day. Perhaps it was an unconventional vision for a seven-year-old, but she "envisioned [herself] being in the corporate world." In fact, she "always wanted to be the boss."

At this time, though, in the early 1980s while she was playing with her dolls, the insurance industry—where she would end up working—was mostly white men. In fact, when Marita Zuraitis, current CEO of Horace Mann Educators Corporation, began her career at Aetna Life in 1982, she was often the only woman in the room (Ross and Woleben 2020). Zuraitis notes, "There really was a very rigid, high number of hours necessary to put in to move ahead" (Ross and Woleben 2020). Overcoming gender disparity in this sector proved difficult because so few women wanted to fight such an uphill battle for an even playing field in the first place.

When Mrs. Tale entered the workforce in the early 2000s, the insurance industry saw a surge in female representation—in fact, over 60 percent of the workforce was comprised of women (STEMconnector 2017). However, women still only held 19 percent of board seats, 11 percent of inside officer roles, and 12 percent of C-suite positions (i.e., CEO, COO, and CFO). Furthermore, 92 percent of insurance companies did not have mandated programs to change this problem and help women develop their careers (STEMconnector 2017).

At the beginning of Mrs. Tale's career, her male coworkers were overly nice, voluntarily taking on the "dad" role and offering their expertise on things she already knew how to do. As a new face to the industry, she was at a loss for how to explain that she didn't appreciate their generosity without sounding offensive and potentially risking her still-developing reputation. She had no choice but to stay quiet.

The decision to stay silent was not always a decision *she* made, though.

Mrs. Tale shared, "I am not a particularly shy person. I have always been loud, but speaking up in meetings was almost impossible." Many of her male coworkers still wanted to treat the women in the room as if they were non-existent. Her suggestions would be drowned out unless a male coworker's voice echoed her idea. Then, suddenly, everyone pretended this was an amazing and, most importantly, *original* idea.

When she did manage to secure the spotlight, her older managers gave each other sidelong glances with disgusted expressions, shocked she would dare to act so greedily and take away time from people *they* deemed deserving to speak. It seemed not once did they feel guilty they were dismissing her thoughts and making it impossible for her to advocate for herself. Even on days she felt particularly brave, she left the workplace with her head hanging low.

She exclaimed to me, "I was called a silly girl who simply wasn't there yet."

I swallowed silently.

Mrs. Tale thought if she could seize any opportunity given to her in the workplace, she would be able to prove her worth—but she was never given any. Even though she held a managerial position at her last job, boasted immense prior experience, and was hired to work in the technical aspects of the industry under her manager's eye, she was treated like his secretary, burdened with tasks far below her pay grade.

She spent entire workdays writing Christmas cards, creating gift inventories, and sorting papers alphabetically into a filing cabinet. Her manager could have easily performed these jobs or had a secretary perform them. But he never did because he knew he could always have her fulfill them. Research conducted by Fisher Phillips from 2010 to 2020 found that female employees are regularly designated the "Office Mom," taking on tasks such as planning parties, restocking office pantries, and ensuring the birthday calendar is filled in (Bifoss 2019).

When she was eventually promoted to a more promising role, Mrs. Tale—despite building an *entire* department from scratch—learned her male coworkers at the same management level were being paid more. She had trained new employees and sacrificed hours of her own time to teach them how to carry on the company's mission. Then, when she tried to complain, management simply turned their heads.

When the COVID-19 pandemic demanded a new virtual model that transitioned everyone from the usual physical interactions to remote meetings, Mrs. Tale found the majority of her job now consisted of phone calls in which her clients could not see her face or body language but simply heard her voice.

She noted, "I had to talk on the phone, and I sound young.""

I agreed, laughing a little. "You do sound like you are barely older than me!"

She acknowledged my compliment and continued, telling me, "I have been doing my job for fifteen years, but I have people (always men) ask to talk to my manager because they don't believe what I am saying." Those particular clients who doubted her advice and answers would be suddenly reassured when her manager repeated everything she had already told them. Usually, they'd have no follow-up or clarifying questions.

And all along, she said nothing in protest.

The silence transitioned into a fiery burnout, making Jenny Tale feel there was no point in giving more effort. Every day felt like a Sisyphean climb—one where her feet slipped and lost their grip just as she almost crossed the finish line and would be forced to start at the same spot the next day. This same girl had dreamed of corporate work, dressed up her Barbies in suits instead of dresses, and believed she could be the boss. Now, she didn't even want to bother. No one, no matter what she did, wanted to hear her.

She asked herself, "Why do I have to give my all to my job when other people do not try nearly as much yet still gain respect and appropriate compensation for their efforts?"

But in this struggle for power and equality in the workplace, she did not give up. Instead, she dedicated a great amount of energy to ensuring the barriers she faced would be minimized for younger generations. Her efforts as a pioneer in the current state of the insurance industry allow for the hope the small percentage of women in leadership roles will grow. She says it is still possible to fulfill our childhood dreams, and a part of her feels that in some ways... she has.

Her experience allowed her to meet other women dealing with the same problems in the finance industry, and she created her own chapter of a national woman's business organization in Philadelphia to facilitate events she wanted to see in her local area. She held seminars on techniques to overcome fear in the workplace and conversation starters for discussions about gender inequality with men.

Mrs. Tale believes the best way to minimize workplace inequality is to ensure women speak up about their struggles. Too many men think that because they do not engage in unequal treatment, the problem does not exist—and so when a *sole* woman voices her concerns, they categorize her as dramatic and turn the other way. However, with thousands of stories, men have no choice but to listen.

Mrs. Tale began inserting many practices she preached in her seminars into her own work life. Slowly, as she proved to herself she *did* have the self-confidence to speak up, she began expressing her ideas during meetings. She was not content in changing just herself, though. She decided to take on a mentorship role, so her days after work gradually became filled with connecting with young men because she didn't want them to see what the older generation was doing and think it was acceptable to continue that behavior.

By fostering connections with them, she helps close the generational gap in the workforce. As older men retire and new, fresh faces enter the employment cycle, Mrs. Tale helps ensure the cycle of negativity she endured is broken by becoming their first friendly connection or mentor to them.

Inspired by her story and resilience, I asked, "Do you have any advice you would like to share with other little girls who have big dreams?"

She answered, "Recognize you *can* do it. It is going to be harder. Be prepared for everything. Feel better than everyone else does because you want to give people the opportunity to critique as few things as possible. I know this is unfair advice, but it is *real* advice."

Mrs. Tale also understands the fine line between giving up and realizing nothing more can be done. It is not weak or lacking in courage to distance oneself from a situation if it is too dangerous to continue on. In fact, it is a sign of bravery. She lives by the mantra: "If you know you cannot change people, leaving is always an option. There is always another place that is better." After all, she left her previous company and now thrives in a workplace that treasures her work and ideas.

When our phone call ended, it took me a while to regain my composure. I had spent so much of my life complaining to my friends and family it wasn't fair I was a girl because my opportunities were so limited—yet this was the first time I had actually sat down with a woman to talk about her experiences. Her story was not a temporary ten-minute video I could fast forward through at will. The events in her life did not just live in my YouTube watch history but in her permanent memory—and now mine too.

I learned from her that dreams are simply dreams. We can choose to lament over our identities and how the world seems to be against us, but we also have the choice to make something inspiring out of the restrictions around us. Our lives are bigger than what we cannot do. Mrs. Tale's words exemplify how even when she lost her voice, she did not lose her heart to fight.

Jenny Tale may not have been able to work in the corner office she envisioned when she was a little girl—but instead she works in Manhattan with a premier view of the city from the highest floor. I am sure, while she would agree with Dhar Mann that some jobs require a skirt, not a suit, she wants everyone to know that women can wear a suit too.

Chapter 9

"They're just a bunch of girls! You're so much smarter than them," the boy said to his debate partner.

As I heard him make that statement, my pen froze mid-sentence—I stared dumbfounded at the boy I used to share my toys with during indoor recess. How could he say something so cruel? About me... about us... to our competitors? All the excitement churning and building inside me over participating in the debate exploded into rage.

It was the week of the highly-anticipated fourth grade debate. I was one of the lucky eight kids selected to represent my class, and we were then evenly split into two groups: girls and boys. I was thrilled to be chosen because, as my family can definitely attest, I loved arguing.

The days leading up to the debate were nerve-wracking, especially with the animosity we received from the boys.

As the pro-group, we had the responsibility of going first. While my friend said her opening statement, I heard the boys snickering, so instead of listening to her I focused my energy on giving them the most intimidating stare my eyes could muster. Eventually, though, it was my turn to rebuttal.

I pulled out my document of numbers and figures and then, looking out at the audience, I froze. For the one minute I was allotted to speak, I said exactly one sentence.

When I left the stage, my friends patted my back sympathetically while our competitors were smacking each other's backs triumphantly. I covered my eyes when their rebuttal person delivered an amazing, eloquent speech.

All the boys in the room erupted in applause.

As with all classroom activities in fourth grade, the teachers didn't pick a winner. They said we tied. But we all knew who took home the trophy.

I think the most troubling part was that these boys were ten years old, some of them nine. Even at that age, they were already predisposed to the attitude they are superior to girls and, therefore, can say mean remarks or make other people feel less than. I felt horrible for days that I had lost, and a part of me thought perhaps they had been right… maybe they were much smarter than I was.

I hadn't thought of that debate in years, but as I interviewed Olivia Thomas, who wishes to remain anonymous, every ounce of frustration, embarrassment, and anger rose to the surface. I was fortunate enough to listen to her unique workplace experiences that I hope will show young women gender inequality should not devalue their hard work and affects everyone—including the very people who may be inflicting it.

As I positioned myself comfortably in my seat, I asked her my famous opening question, "What was your dream as a little girl?"

Thomas let out a soft sigh and said, "Wow, that is such a good question. I don't know that I had a specific job I wanted to do, but I definitely loved learning."

This yearning for knowledge still manifests in her present day-to-day life. She does not have a typical job but rather is able to do what she loves—whether researching for her books or simply gathering statistics on the ever-changing workplace.

"Children should find something they want to do regardless if an employer pays them or not," she emphasized.

This really stuck with me.

During first period on the first day of eleventh grade, my teacher passed out index cards so we could write down what we wanted to be when we grew up. The majority of my classmates wrote down a career: doctor, engineer, astronaut, lawyer, computer programmer, dancer.

Very few of us jotted down an adjective like happy or content. And it scared me slightly that we were already defining our lives by a job—not what would bring us fulfillment.

Thomas believes her adoration for learning sets her apart. So, when her femininity made her a target early in her career, she not only persevered… she learned from the experience so she could share it with others.

On her first day as a manager at a new job, as people bustled around slapping loaves of salty bread on sliced tomatoes and devouring bowls of creamy spinach pasta in the cafeteria, Thomas walked in, fanning her face as the rush of warm air from the ventilators permeated the room.

Suddenly she heard her name. Her boss standing on the opposite side of the room yelled, "Hey, Olivia! You're a woman. Why don't you wash the dishes?" It was one of the first sentences he had ever said to her.

Thomas's heart sank. At that moment she thought, *I'm never going to be accepted here. How could my boss treat me this way?* Part of her felt devalued because she saw the interactions between her boss and her male colleagues. They were vastly different from the way he had just treated her.

Still, Thomas turned around, looked at her boss, and said with her voice breaking slightly, "Hey, you've got two hands. Why don't *you* wash the dishes?"

Immediately, her boss became furious. He snarled, "This is why I hate working with women. They can't take a joke."

Thomas would remember this conversation for years. But I was surprised to learn her reason for remembering this centered on the emotions of other people, not just hers.

While Thomas concedes this experience negatively affected her mental health, she also pointed out that "the people witnessing those moments—it also detrimentally affects *their* mental and emotional well-being because no one wants to see a colleague being discriminated against."

According to a National Library of Medicine study on how bystanders react to workplace discrimination, those who observe inequality and sense they, too, may one day be in the same position feel threatened and have extreme reactions (Sinclair 2021). Another study conducted by Elkins, Phillips, and Konopaske discovered that when many female witnesses see someone being discriminated against, they see themselves also becoming victims (Sinclair 2021).

The studies underscore this point by emphasizing no colleague wants to see one of their coworkers being mistreated, as it alerts them they might be subject to this type of behavior, too, sometime in the future for a factor they are unable to control—which may not even be gender. It signals this is not a safe workplace, and seeing a victim of discrimination just highlights that perhaps their emotional well-being and even physical safety may be impacted too.

While reading about this I thought, *Why don't more people call out moments of inequality, then?* If it affects everyone, not only the person on the receiving end of discrimination, shouldn't everyone be more inclined to protest?

When I asked Thomas that question, she answered, "It is a privilege to have the ability to call out inequality because discrimination can never be solved."

We live in an imperfect world.

In fact, she admitted "it cost [her]" when she spoke up because her boss did not recognize his mistake and continued speaking to her in a demeaning manner. She had already been devalued in front of a large group of people, and his continued insults made it difficult to regain her composure.

Perhaps he will never realize what he did to her.

The silver lining in her story is that, after the cafeteria encounter with her boss, some of her male colleagues approached her and told her how disgusted they were with the way she had been treated. Many stated they wanted to speak up on her behalf but could not find the courage. Still, their interest in working at the company dwindled from witnessing unfair behavior.

Inequality didn't *only* hurt Thomas. It affected everyone in the company differently. This realization spurred her to dream of a workplace that celebrates everyone's differences, where everyone feels comfortable speaking up when people do not follow through on those values.

In fact, Thomas emphasized, "Even though a company may make a mistake in trying to achieve equality, it is how they are able to learn from those experiences and find methods that prevent the error from occurring which is important."

She wants everyone to recognize it does not have to be the woman—who has just been emotionally damaged—to say something. Rather, everyone in the company has the ability to call it out because speaking up helps everyone. She says, "In a workplace where I am free to be myself because I will be valued for that means you are free to be yourself and be valued for that."

In the end, when corporate management creates an environment where everyone is treated equally, regardless of background, people feel more comfortable sharing their opinions. Knowing they are valued and are safe to express their feelings, they can engage in six practices: developing new ideas, ensuring everyone is heard, properly attributing ownership to ideas, offering constructive criticism, implementing that feedback, and then allowing employees under management to make decisions. This then results in employees being three and a half times as likely to share their ingenious ideas and contribute to a productive work environment in which workforce diversity results in creativity, not inequality (Hewlett, Marshall, and Sherbin 2013).

I then proceeded to a topic targeting the foundational issues with the workplace: It was developed with men in mind, not women.

Thomas agreed, recounting, "Too many times, women see this mistreatment and immediately think, 'What can I do to change to fit into this work environment?' instead of asking, 'How can the work environment change to accommodate me?'"

This resonated with me. I grew up hearing from all our elementary school teachers that every one of us had a unique talent, that we each brought something new to the table.

"We need to deviate from the ideal worker," Thomas said passionately.

Women have their own distinctive capabilities they bring to the table, which companies can use to thrive. Unfortunately, these differences are too seldom celebrated.

At one of her jobs, Thomas discovered she was pregnant with her first child. She promptly reached out to her chief financial officer to ask for unpaid leave for four months.

Frustrated, he looked at her and said, "This is why I don't like hiring women. They just go off and have babies."

Her manager had similar opinions, repeatedly guilting her that this four-month leave was the most they had ever awarded anyone. It seemed as if they wanted Thomas to feel her demand was excessive, yet their company was *generous enough* to honor it.

When she became pregnant again, at another workplace this time, Thomas was forced to purchase both short-term disability insurance and health insurance under her employer to cover her leave from work. She was not provided paid or unpaid maternity leave.

I consider myself a "personal finance nerd," and at hearing this my eyes immediately widened. Thomas was now responsible for double the insurance premiums, and her pregnancy was considered a short-term disability… likened to an injury that left her temporarily unable to work.

It wasn't just her, though. Thomas recounts how she worked with a woman expecting twins who had a cesarean instead of a normal delivery. Her coworker was ecstatic because this meant she now had six weeks off from work.

Thomas remarked, "That is outrageous. A six-week old baby needs her mother. You get absolutely no sleep the first six months you have a child, let alone two children. Every parent knows that."

I couldn't help but wonder: If every parent knows that, then why have so many stayed silent in the fight for paid maternity leave? Why do so many pregnant women feel compelled to hide their bumps so other people in their workplace do not realize?

But it isn't just new mothers trying to understand how to best raise their children and manage their work. It is new fathers as well. In fact, when men ask to leave work for a period of time for family reasons, they are hurt professionally more than women. According to the World Economic Forum, 20 percent of men believe if they were to take paternity leave, it would greatly affect their careers and make it almost impossible for them to come back to the same situation they left (Janjuha-Jivraj 2023).

It seems like workplaces honor only those who are able to commit *all* their time to their work and make it their number one priority. If they want to cut their work hours, even for something as necessary as pregnancy, America paints them as someone who deviates from the ideal worker or is not responsible enough.

Thomas recognizes that some organizations do now provide maternity, paternity, and adoption leave for their employees. However, because it is not mandated by the government through legislation, other workplaces are not taking the initiative to also incorporate these benefits.

She told me, "It isn't just about children—it is about dependent care. It is about people wanting to integrate their work and interests…"

More often than not, there is no distinction between work and home life. The *bare* minimum is to respect that people cannot always devote their full attention to their job, then help them manage their time instead of burdening them with more responsibility.

Paid maternity leave is not a benefit or short-term disability. It is a human need so people can ensure their emotional and physical health thrives and, when they do come back to the workplace, they are then ready to commit time and energy to their jobs.

Thomas poses the question, "Who wants an employee who consecutively has two or three hours of sleep at night doing anything in their office?"

It is obvious a common theme in her own answers is that *everyone* is affected by gender inequality, including the very companies inhibiting women from recharging efficiently. Now half the workforce is actually productive, while the other half is unenergized and dragging down the staff.

I cannot help but think that Thomas's heated encounter with her boss and unfortunate experiences with asking for maternity leave are inevitable. We have to accept that such moments will exist—but we cannot simply accept the workplace where this discrimination occurs.

Thomas suggests asking ourselves if this is an organization where we will be able to grow… or an organization where we can be ourselves.

The workplace is more than just our job. She fondly emphasized, "It is a place where most of the time we are awake is spent."

I nodded my head and added, "It is one of the first places where our minds wander to when we wake up from a dream, and where we gain most of our experiences and stories to tell."

If we are changing ourselves to fit into that particular company, then we are limiting our own success when it isn't a workplace that truly values us. Thomas wants every person, gender aside, to be able to leave that environment and navigate to a place where their salaries are just an added benefit, not a main motivating factor.

So for Thomas, the idea that fulfilling our childhood dreams is impossible is frankly preposterous. She posited, "I think we often devalue the process of trying, and there is this obsession right now with success and failure."

Everything we do ends up as either success or failure. But the people who really accomplish something beautiful in their lives are the ones who enjoy the process itself. Life is more than just our goals. She thinks too many people measure their lives in simply goals and are so focused on the end prize they miss the journey. They never take the time to enjoy life—it is just achievement after achievement for them.

For Thomas, what she loves and enjoys comes in the form of writing books—and she wishes to write many more. She enjoys sharing what she has learned with other people.

Talking to Olivia Thomas made me realize I have spent so much of my life doing just that: drafting up goals and checking them off based on my performance. When I "lost" the debate in front of my class, I measured my success based on a victory and other people's reactions. Yet the process of preparing for a debate, gathering statistics, hearing my friends speak with passion—all of that was immediately flushed down the moment I messed up. Instead of treasuring the journey of creating, I lamented the loss of destroying my opponent.

All of those women in the workplace who faced inequality, and who still struggle with discrimination today, are people who wanted to learn and pursue a career. Thomas traveled across the world in pursuit of new opportunities. The woman who gave birth to twins loved her job so much she juggled her career with two tiny six-week-old babies. These difficult, inequitable moments became a part of their journey. Perhaps they never thought they would achieve their goals if the world was really so against them, but they still forged on.

If these women could get back up from a moment where they were knocked down so brutally, then could I not also take comments from just a bunch of tiny nine-year-old boys?

Olivia Thomas taught me there is nothing wrong with me—it's the society we have grown up in. Now it's our generation's responsibility to slowly fix it.

Some believe the discussion of inequality has become "over-talked about," but in my opinion it's not talked about enough. The more I research and discuss, the more I learn. Now I know why Olivia Thomas likes learning so much.

Chapter 10

———

When I was five years old, my family attended our neighbor's annual Diwali party. We were all excited for a night of festivities—eating Indian delicacies that melted in our mouths, trading exciting stories with our friends, and of course, standing outside in the freezing November darkness with sparklers in our hands. I remember arriving at their house in a beautiful traditional Indian dress: I was clutching my sister, who was just a couple of months old in her tiny rocker and eager to spend her first Diwali together.

The next two hours were, as always, a whirlwind of enjoyment. We ran around the house, almost knocking over dinner platters set on the table, and giggled every time an exasperated adult came to quiet us down. We buried our hands in salty potato chips as we watched Bollywood movies and tried to copy the dance moves on the screen while failing miserably.

My favorite part, though, was when the fireworks started. And this year, I was finally old enough to hold the sparkler all by myself instead of my dad hovering next to me.

When the time came, I was the first person out the door and into the garage where a box of sparklers and firecrackers lay open.

As my friend's dad retrieved a sparkler from the cart and gave it to me, he cautioned, "Remember, Simran, be careful. Fire is hot. You can severely burn yourself."

I nodded my head earnestly and took the stick from him, but inside my head thoughts screamed in disbelief. All my life, people had been telling me this transparent, orange flame was somehow capable of searing through my skin and leaving permanent scars. Yet, I had never touched it. I blindly trusted them.

It was especially cold that day—so cold that even my soft winter jacket did not shield me from the piercing winter chill. Yet the heat emanating from the sparkler in my hand was enticingly warm. And in that moment, I decided I would see if fire really *was* hot or if every adult in my life was in on some kind of inside joke and I their gullible victim.

I grabbed onto the other side of the sparkler, the part where tiny orange stubs were flickering on the stick as tendrils of smoke traveled into the air. I held on to it for approximately thirty-seven seconds before releasing the loudest, most blood-curdling scream my body could possibly summon. The palm of my left hand felt as if a bed of needles had stabbed it—and no matter how hard I shook it, the burning sensation would not leave.

My dad came running to me, asking what was wrong, but the fire had somehow removed my voice from my throat and the only thing I could do was continue screaming. In the short five years I had been alive, I had never felt such horrible pain in my life. And the sole thought running in my head was: *Why did I not just listen to everyone's warnings?*

Seven years later, in middle school during our personal narratives unit, my English teacher brought up the importance of experience and how there are two types of people: one who believes it when they hear fire is hot, and the other who has to burn themselves to understand. For the latter, no matter how many people try to protect them, they will realize the danger only after they have been through it. But they mature.

Now that I know the dangers of fire, I stand by my sister during these Diwali parties and ensure she does not make the same mistake. I do not want her to go through the same pain I did.

I was lucky enough to have had people warn me, though. Some people have to become the one who warns everyone else.

And, of course, someone had to touch fire and severely burn themselves for the rest of us to know to avoid it.

The power of these memories hit me when I was given the amazing opportunity to video call Amelia Weller, an African American female government official who is also in the midst of writing a book about gender inequality. Her name has been changed to protect her privacy.

She had no idea what fire she was getting into by entering the workforce, but not only did she bravely fight through the flames, but she used her experience to ensure those who walk through the blaze behind her come out with fewer scars.

She did this not just for her, but for us too.

I opened up the interview as usual: "What was your dream as a little girl, Mrs. Weller?"

Unlike interviewees who needed some time to answer the question, she answered immediately. And she did not have just one dream, she had two.

Her first aspiration was to become a dancer.

She reminisced, "Something about twirling across the dance floor made me feel free." She felt as if she could jump across the sky with just her pointe shoes.

As she aged a little, she moved on to envision a more practical career—becoming a lawyer, specifically a criminal defense-attorney. She saw herself in the courtroom, fighting to uphold equality and making a difference in other people's lives when they feel there's no more life to live.

Instead, she ended up working in the aviation industry for the government.

"It is a very much male-dominated work environment," she said, raising her eyebrows slightly. I immediately knew the direction this interview would be heading.

Although the number of female leaders in government is increasing, they are still vastly underrepresented. According to data collated by the UN, women comprise only 22.8 percent of head Cabinet members (Pew Research Center 2018).

And so, despite working in the government—the entity that people look up to to foster equality and overturn injustice—Mrs. Weller faced many challenges over being taken seriously as a woman, especially one without a technical background since she majored in marketing and communication.

"My coworkers were all men and either air traffic controllers or engineers who only listened to each other because they didn't think I was qualified enough to offer an opinion," she shared. "They would do what Gen Z calls 'mansplaining.'"

Weller described how conversations became their opportunity to reiterate everything she already knew.

"They would define leader to me! Even though I was an executive." Weller laughed.

When she did not provide her coworkers every detail about what she had done or said in a particular situation, they simply assumed she hadn't thought to do it.

"It was frustrating to hear, 'Well, did you also do this?' and 'Or shouldn't you also have done that?' when I did in fact do all those things. All my hard work would go unnoticed because I did not include them in my debrief," Mrs. Weller said disappointedly.

It happened so often she had to adjust her communication style to prevent those follow-up conversations from occurring.

Weller couldn't help but feel, though, her lack of technical expertise was not why she was ignored. It was because of the demographic boxes she checked. Both labels—African American and woman—caused her to differ greatly from the standard image of an "ideal" worker.

But she wasn't alone in this treatment.

A report compiled for the Royal Aeronautical Society by Carol Anderson, a well-established board member in the International Aviation Women's Association, says, "Although girls work very hard at school and university and achieve great results often outperforming their male counterparts, that initial advantage seems to disappear the moment they graduate into their professional careers, especially in the male-dominated world of aviation"(Szakal 2019). Anderson believes this can be attributed to the minimal number of female leaders in the particular industry. Without that precedent in place, many of the younger generation do not know how to advocate for themselves (Szakal 2019).

At a previous workplace within the private sector, Weller had men touch her in a way that made her uncomfortable, even though they did not have the intention of harassing her.

"Yet that was exactly what was happening," she emphasized. "They would approach me at my desk and start rubbing my shoulders or placing their hand on my lower back—which made me noticeably uneasy." When she finally found the courage to speak up for herself, her career and any advancement opportunities in that specific company were completely destroyed. She had to pick up her bags and leave.

For years, she overlooked the inequality in her work life because she was afraid of the consequences—especially after she lost her job for reporting inappropriate physical contact from some of the men.

"I thought I would get in trouble any time I spoke up," she admitted.

But she didn't feel good about herself anymore.

"I felt terrible about how I was letting people mistreat me. If I didn't speak up for myself, who would speak up on behalf of me?" she asked.

I agreed. Perhaps she would never know for certain if she could change the outcome, but she still had a voice to keep trying. She couldn't keep coming to work and doing things that made her feel uncomfortable, and she certainly didn't want little girls to grow up and hate themselves for the way others treated them either.

After a particularly troubling day at the workplace, she sat down and tried to understand what her values were. Then she wrote them down. These were tenets she categorized as important and would never compromise on, such as authenticity and integrity.

Once she pinpointed those principles, she made a list of what "sat well" for her and what frankly did not. This exercise may have been brief, but now whenever she felt self-doubt in a situation, she could think carefully on whether the decision aligned with her values. If it did not, she would find or create another way to overcome it.

She looked at me with a slight smile on her face, then said, "It is the ideas of the upcoming generations that we need for the future, but not all of us are comfortable embracing them." We have to become comfortable with being uncomfortable—because if we shy away from speaking up, we will just continue silently suffering.

Weller shared some advice she received from her coach as well: "*We* teach people how to treat us. The moment we allow mistreatment, it becomes our responsibility. *We* have to be the ones to show others how we want to be dealt with professionally, in a respectful manner."

I was moved by this wisdom and also comforted by it. Weller reminded me that, through our choices, we always have at least some control over discriminatory situations. Now when people silence Weller in a meeting, she ensures they come back to her idea. Even if they are about to wrap up the discussion, she will fight to make it a minute longer so she can share or at least put it at the beginning of the next meeting's agenda.

"I now refuse to let people get away with their mistreatment, because by accepting it I become a part of that inequality," she told me fiercely.

However, Amelia Weller also wants everyone to know that although it is necessary to speak up and overcome the fear of advocating for oneself, it is also necessary to give people grace and show compassion.

She says, "The people who are part of these structures and systems that end up preventing little girls from being what they want to be or making their journeys extremely difficult did not set out to do that. That was not their childhood dream: to destroy other little girls' dreams."

The problem is they are just doing what they have always known—because of the systematic biases that plague our world. It has become our societal responsibility to change the framework of knowledge passed onto the next male generation.

"We cannot find peace in just passing the guilt on to a select group of men. We should instead try to change the world which caused them to turn out this way," she said powerfully.

And she did just that. When Weller was in Atlanta as a director at another company, one of the components of her job description was to sign off each time her team hired a new person. It became apparent, however, they were only hiring white men over the age of fifty, even though the group already consisted of the same demographic.

Weller was troubled: All these people possessed the same background. They had the same perspectives. They had the same thoughts. They did not have unique experiences. There was no thinking outside the box.

After seeing virtually no progress in the company, she changed one small part of the hiring process. No longer would the team be allowed to see people's names or where they were from. They could only view their résumés with a list of qualifications.

Suddenly, just like that, the team was hiring women. They were bringing in younger white and Black men. They even had an Asian man!

As she should, Mrs. Weller reveled in the fact there was now so much diversity in the company. Human resources could now only focus on how qualified a particular person is rather than recognizing a name they knew—such as their cousin or a nephew or someone they worked with ten years ago—and allowing them to rise above the surface.

However, just to verify her decision had been the correct one, Weller asked her white manager what he thought of all these new people.

She questioned, "Do you feel like you are missing something? Do you feel like your choices are poor ones? How do you feel about how your team is starting to look different?"

And he responded, "I am happy with the change. I feel empowered with the new energy they bring in. They are more productive. They create quality products for the customers, and now they love us more!"

Eventually, when that male manager retired, a younger Black woman replaced him. This was the first time in their history that a Black woman—or any woman, for that matter—led that particular team.

Weller also found solace in Chief, a woman's networking organization for senior leaders. This was a place for women to band together and create a support system to endure difficult challenges.

"I love how each woman, separately, may be the only woman in their respective room, sitting alone at their meetings, but when they come together in one room they become a force to reckon with," she described adoringly.

So what happens when all those women are in one room together?

Chief prides itself on its confidentiality because many of these women hold very important positions. The friends they make through these organizations do not broadcast their problems, thereby formulating an environment of both venting and healing. Chief also brings in influential people from all over the world to talk about their experiences, like Melinda Gates, Eva Longoria, and even Michelle Obama, who are excited to share their insights with an eager group of women.

Structurally, Chief is broken down into smaller organizations: ones for Latino women, African American women, female authors, and even women who live in Washington, DC, like Amelia Weller.

"The women are all so wonderful and are ready to offer any assistance they can—like résumé help or coaching in a certain situation," she detailed. I immediately knew that once I was senior enough at a company, I would try to join.

Chief additionally tries to foster a connection with younger generations, specifically women just about to enter the workforce, so they can pass on the knowledge Weller says she wishes she knew sooner.

And despite Amelia Weller not becoming a dancer or criminal defense attorney, she still believes it is possible to fulfill our childhood dreams. She just did not know herself well enough back then to answer such a broad question of what she wanted to be when she grew up.

Like the other interviewees, she wants to steer little girls to what brings them happiness and excitement—so they can learn early-on life is all about fulfillment and feeling content with themselves.

"Achieving our dreams is within us," she says. "If we truly want to get where we want to be, then we will be able to get over any roadblocks we might encounter."

Listening to Amelia Weller made me aware of my struggle to see the world from others' perspectives. I could never really take a moment to consider how different everyone's experiences are. How many other teenagers can tell their friends they know fire is hot because they have held it in their hand for thirty-seven seconds before? Not the majority. Yet we still, as a collective community, know we shouldn't touch it.

Every woman has a unique tale to tell about her struggles in the workplace. Their experiences have forced them to reconcile with the common knowledge that gender inequality is not a thing of the past—just like we know fire burns.

I am quick to label men who hinder women's pursuit of success as villains, but I don't know their stories. I only know mine. But when women support each other, they learn to see the world through other lenses, including men's.

Gender inequality should not be a mandatory rite of passage for all women. No woman should have to go to her workplace and start to hate herself because she is complacent despite being mistreated. But if we let those experiences be our defining moments and let our stories boil down to just the hurt, then that inequality will become a thing of the future too.

The beauty of a burn is that, in the moment, there is so much pain—but now I can only imagine what it felt like. Amelia Weller believes our burns are what make us stronger and teach us lessons that words only scratch the surface of.

No one warned Weller when she entered the workforce. She came out, not unscathed but with warnings… and most importantly with experience and wisdom. It would do all of us good to listen.

Chapter 11

I have heard the phrase "Do it for your sister, mother, aunt, and grandmother" directed to countless men, but writing this book has taught me to think differently. Men should do it for themselves.

As the sun bathed the world in gleaming, golden light, I sat on the park bench with a popsicle dripping in my hands, thinking about just that. Little boys and girls played all around, running through sprinklers and screaming when the cool jet of water splashed their bare feet. Some used stubs of chalk, barely bigger than their small palms, to draw the outlines of a four square game on the pavement. Others ran up and down the slide, pushing each other out of the way, frantically waiting for their turn, and screaming when unable to shove their way through.

Watching them made me nostalgic. I wanted to go back to a simpler time, back when the large stack of assignments piling up on my dashboard was non-existent and I could run around aimlessly and free without that panicked feeling I forgot to do something.

What I missed the most, though, was not their care-free life-styles but their innocence. The unspoken truth about education is that while we are presented the beautiful opportunity to learn about things we never knew, we are also exposed to the world's ugliness. We learn about wars, bombings, inequality—all of which built the very playground they now run around on.

It terrifies me how quickly those parks transform into the kind of workplaces Aileen Rizo, Reema, Jenny Tale, Amelia Weller, and Olivia Thomas battled through every day. After all, years ago, they too played on slides, pushing the boys out of their way for their turn. They had boy versus girl water gun fights. They fought over who would be king or queen in their small four square games. But when those boys traded their play clothes for business suits, it was never the same again—and the girls were sent to the back of the line for every activity.

It does not have to be this way. Those girls and boys playing in that park don't have to grow up and experience those struggles. Because gender inequality does not affect just women like Rizo, Reema, Tale, Weller, and Thomas, it affects boys and men too.

All those women made sure to emphasize to me that workplace gender inequality is not only a woman's struggle, but a man's too.

I did not understand that before.

After all, we have always been advocating for women's rights: Women could not vote until the 1900s. We still have never had a female president. Rizo was paid less than a man she was more qualified and experienced than for the same work. Reema was forced to sacrifice any remaining hopes of a job to take care of her children. Tale was given Christmas cards to write and silenced at every meeting. Weller faced sexual advances and was thrown out of her position when she spoke up. Thomas was told to wash the dishes in front of an entire lunchroom because she was a woman. How exactly are men affected here?

A part of me, I think, was selfish. The fight for equal workplaces was a chance for women to prove they are deserving, and I could not possibly imagine how their struggles—which, to me, are so profoundly troubling—could be something men faced too.

In all the movements Rizo, Reema, Tale, Weller, and Thomas were a part of, they tried enlisting men to help bring change to the world. Countless men told them, "This isn't my problem. I don't treat women this way." To that, each of these women made sure to show them how gender inequality was still their issue, because they may not have been the perpetrator, but in some way they were still a victim of a severe imbalance in justice.

I long for my childhood almost every day. I cannot count how many times I have enviously gazed out the window and saw all the little kids—knee-deep in mud, playing in my backyard—while I sat at my desk researching and writing. But some day those kids will grow up and potentially read this book, seeking knowledge.

Because as much as I want them to play forever, I also recognize there comes a turnover period where they must
shed their obliviousness and learn about the framework of
the world women have been trying to tear down and build
anew for the past several generations. I think it is even more
important to realize we have the ability and power to still
change minds—especially in those who are younger than
we are and learn through practice of what is right and what
is wrong.

I continually look at my sister to remind myself of the number
of people who are dependent on us to enforce positive change,
including my male cousins, who seem to already be placing
the hat of responsibility on their heads to become "the man."
I forgot that society often expects men to be emotionless
and independent, barring them from many predominately
female-occupied positions because the latter are not "manly"
enough. I mean, if we do not even recognize that men face
issues too, then how will we ever help them?

Gender inequality is not just a problem for women. It is a
matter for men too. So, I push forward in my efforts for an
equal playing field between women and men—not just for
women's sake. I hope the next few pages will illustrate why
this is so necessary.

Chapter 12

It took me until the end of my book to realize that while I preached for gender equality, I had only taken primary and secondary accounts from women—thus engaging in the very same bias I accused others of. And with that awareness, I remembered a little boy from fifth grade.

It was 2017. I was slowly packing up my stuff and putting it into my bag as the rest of the students trickled out of the room. I was just struggling to find the last school book I had pulled out to skim during silent reading when I heard a kid's soft sniffles also still lingering in the room.

I looked up and doubled over in shock as I saw the "toughest" guy in our class hunched over by the teacher's desk, sobbing into her shirt while my teacher patted him on the back. Every ten seconds after taking a shaky breath, he would mumble some words, and the teacher would nod sympathetically and pat his back more, while I… unabashedly… attempted to eavesdrop into the conversation

I don't know how long I stayed unnoticed in the room, but suddenly the boy pulled his head out of her shirt and made direct eye contact as he blinked his tears away. When he saw me, I gave him the world's most sheepish smile while he quickly wiped the remaining evidence he was ever crying from his now-nastily glaring face.

There was the boy I knew.

I recall shoving the rest of my stuff into my backpack and sprinting out of the room, not caring I had failed to find my book but more terrified of what he would do to me now that I had caught him in his most vulnerable moment. After all, we all believed he was not even capable of tears.

It was recess, and my friends and I were playing on the swings when he shuffled over and beckoned me to follow. Slightly nervous but also bubbling with curiosity, I jumped off of my swing and ran after him. When we were a respectable distance from everyone else, he loomed down at me threateningly (he was already four inches taller) and said, "If you tell anyone, and I mean anyone, a single thing about what happened this morning, I will ruin your life." I gulped nervously, nodded vigorously, and sprinted for the second time that day.

I had grown up with this boy all of elementary school. In third grade, I looked to the side of the room in the midst of a spelling test when he was unfortunately to the right of me—and he yelled to our teacher, "Simran is cheating off of me!" In fifth grade, I still believed in Santa, and when I showed up to school in my festive pajamas, bubbling with holiday spirit, he informed me the mystical man I had spent every Christmas Eve painstakingly baking cookies for was none other than my father. He laughed hysterically as I cried. Also in fifth grade, when I lost my jacket and mittens and had to walk outside in the freezing cold in my thin sweater, I realized, with my fingers blue and teeth chattering, they were in his cubby.

Never once did I think there was something or someone who could make him cry—he had made it his life mission to bring misery to his other classmates.

That's why I will never forget how ashamed this boy was for his mistakenly seen fit of tears in front of me. We never talked about it again, but it always lingered in the room. I am sure he worried that if people realized he was capable of being vulnerable, his manly reputation would be disintegrated.

I realized his behavior toward me and the other girls was not because he was a bad person: he lived in genuine fear if he did not exercise his "masculine superiority" toward other people, then everyone would laugh and point at him, saying, "You cry like a girl."

When gender inequality falls apart, men can break away from constrictive societal standards that prevent them from being free and happy. In her TED talk, Chimamanda Ngozi Adichie discusses how, from a young age, boys are taught to be afraid of fear, weakness, and bury their selves deep within their hearts (Adichie 2013).

Why are boys always the one to pay even if the girl has more money handy in her pocket? Why are girls told they can have ambition but not too much ambition in fear that they may make another man feel inferior (Adichie 2013)?

It is because men have been raised to suppress their emotions from a very young age—taught to hold an "assertive public self"—that whenever they have certain feelings, they won't allow themselves to bring them to surface. When they transition to adulthood, this suppression of emotions carries forward, and when they do slip up and share their feelings they are called "weak" and "a failure" (Essig and Soparnot 2019).

For the first time in my research, I decided to watch what a man had to say about gender inequality to understand men's perspective more. Sociologist Michael Kimmel captured my attention from the moment he began his TED talk. He recalled a defining point in his life—when he and eleven other women convened to have discussions on feminist theory over a potluck dinner. In particular, he remembers a conversation between a white and Black woman (Kimmel 2015).

The white woman began by saying, "All women face the same oppression."

The Black woman disagreed and decided to bring up a question with a puzzled tone. "When you wake up in the morning and you look in the mirror, what do you see?"

The white woman said, "I see a woman."

The Black woman shook her head and decided to answer the question herself: "You see, that is the problem for me. Because when I wake up in the morning and I look in the mirror, I see a Black woman. To me, race is visible. But to you, race is invisible. You don't see it. That is how privilege works. Privilege is invisible to those who have it."

Watching this, Kimmel realized that when he woke up in the morning and looked in the mirror, he did not see his gender: He simply glimpsed a human being. As a middle-class white man, he perceived no race, gender, or even class. He was, as he put it, "universally generalizable." The privilege he possessed was invisible to his own eyes because he navigated no extra barriers in life. Yet many fail to recognize this mindset.

Every other semester, Kimmel alternated teaching a gender sociology course with a female colleague. One day, when he went to give a guest lecture for her course, one of her male students called out in front of everyone, "Oh, finally! An objective opinion." It troubled him that some of those male students in her class believed her gender inequality teachings were biased, because when they saw her, they saw first and foremost a woman. When they saw Kimmel, they saw a human being merely stating facts (Kimmel 2015). That's why Kimmel believes it is crucial every man understands their sheer privilege—because many live their entire lives without ever considering how the women in the room feel. It is more than just feelings and opinions—it is cold fact.

In fact, Kimmel's Ted talk is targeted to the men who believe gender equality is a personal attack against them. He recounts a time when he was on a television show, *A Black Woman Stole My Job*, with four angry white men fuming and trading stories of how they had been in the running for promotions or jobs and were beat out by women.

Kimmel remembers just asking one question about the word "my" in the title: "Where did you get the idea it was already *your* job?" That sense of entitlement, he stresses, is the reason why men continue to be roadblocks against the movement for gender equality—because they are so used to being on the higher end of the uneven playing field. Now, the idea that the power they have could be lessened even a little bit terrifies them. They are afraid if women are finally given the chance to prove themselves, the slight advantage they had before will be gone, and it really will come down to who is better (Kimmel 2015).

That is why women must now show men that gender equality is actually not detrimental to them—they can also benefit from it. It is proven that when women and men are treated equally, companies have higher levels of happiness and, on the other hand, lower job turnover. They do not have to waste their energy in recruiting more employees because the ones they have retained are knowledgeable and efficient.

Of course, there are several inherent biases in workplaces against men, too, not just women. Many organizations do not openly support the idea of paternity leave or part-time work for men, and when these fathers do ask, other coworkers—usually male—judge them. It is not uncommon for phrases such as, "I guess you are not committed to your career, are you?" or "We'll put you on the 'daddy track'" to be thrown as ammunition after such a request (Essig and Soparnot 2019). In fact, employers categorize these men as unqualified workers, and they can even become at risk of losing their jobs or taken out of the running for promotions. Sometimes, they are not considered at all for rewards (Essig and Soparnot 2019).

As a result, men feel pressured to work very long hours, travel wherever, whenever, or however necessary even when they may not have the energy to do so, and try constantly to reach really difficult deadlines—all of which leads to poor work-life balance (Essig and Soparnot 2019). When they are not able to exercise a healthy lifestyle, they are more stressed, less satisfied with their job, and can even experience burnout and mental exhaustion (Essig and Soparnot 2019). In fact, in a study conducted with thirty-three men, twenty-seven shared they worked for more than a combined forty hours every week and felt trapped in a vicious cycle of responsibility because they believed it was their responsibility to live up to "society's unrealistic expectations" (Essig and Soparnot 2019).

This can all result in men holding very negative, depressing thoughts—and with no emotional support system to help when they have these problems, their quality of life is severely depreciated. Especially because it is not as common for men to seek help when needed or even baseline communicate their issues with others, they might be at increased risk of those negative thoughts building to urges of self-harm or suicide (State Government of Victoria 2021).

Although it is very important to acknowledge everything women have done for our society and the strides we have made, it is equally as crucial to realize that getting closer to gender equality is not possible if men do not contribute as well. Women are a powerhouse on their own. Their force is seemingly unmatchable, and they continue to fight year after year with that same renewed energy that, although it burns out at certain points, comes back even stronger. But to make that fire even bigger, men *must* join the movement. The problems are just too rooted in our society.

The first thing they should do is what Michael Kimmel did in front of the mirror: reflect on the privilege they have had since the moment they were born and all the different things they are able to do or don't have to do simply because of a characteristic. As they look at themselves, they should consider how much they've been able to accomplish in life and the number of doors they were able to open simply because people like them have always kept the keys (Menengage 2020).

A common misconception is that for true change to be made, we must have each person engage in action. Instead, men should first listen. Just listen. They should attend and observe changes in women's behavior, and if their female colleagues discuss concerns about the way they have been treated or stories where gender inequality existed, they should not interject or attempt to devalue those incidents (Menengage 2020).

Additionally, as women fight to be equal partners in the workplace, men should make more of an effort to be an equal domestic partner, completing their fair share of the household chores and taking care of the children instead of forcing the woman in the house to do it on her own. We have seen how many women are forced to put work in the backseat because of their home life. If we split those tasks in half, than everyone can prioritize a healthier work-life balance. Men should also advocate for paid leave for *all* people—whether it be maternity or paternity or whatever else. Women have fought to remove themselves from being automatically associated as a cooking and cleaning "traditional caregiver," but oftentimes they are still expected to complete those tasks along with work that men should also be equally involved in (Menengage 2020).

Sometimes I wish I could go back to fifth grade, just to tell that little boy it is okay to cry. At ten years old, he was already taking on the responsibilities of a grown man—suppressing his emotions because he was afraid others would think his tears weak.

I don't think he understood that I did not look at those tears and immediately change my opinion of him. It was not that he no longer wielded strength, rather he actually had feelings and was not an emotionless bully. He became a *person* that day, and I think more men need to realize that by supporting the movement for gender equality, they too can break free from their emotionless shells and become people. Societal workplace pressures are a reflection of our country's inherent belief that men are not allowed to be weak. They must be their family's breadwinners, but they simply cannot engage in household care because it is just not masculine enough. Those standards must be broken down so true gender equality can be obtained—not just for women but men too.

Conclusion

I have always had a difficult time voicing my thoughts. Growing up, I would practice saying "here" silently in my head because there were days when attendance was the only time I spoke in class. I could never figure out how to politely disagree with people, so I would just nod my head slowly and invisibly wince in discomfort. Even now, I would rather swallow hot desert air with a parched throat than raise my hand and ask to get a quick sip at the water fountain.

Deciding to write this book was one of the hardest choices I have ever made. While seeing my name published in a manuscript, flipping through pages of words I ultimately own, and adding *author* to my bio on LinkedIn are all tempting, they were not my primary motivators. I knew going into this process that as a junior in high school, there would be days where I would spend every waking hour trying to write a history paper and have no words left for a book. I was well aware of how tough it would be to fulfill the roles of student during the day and author at night. After all, books are not written in three hours (unlike some of my English essays). But where there is a will, there is a way. I was tired of being underestimated merely because I am a girl. I was exhausted from seeing the hurt faces when my little sister and her friends realized their ideas would always be laughed at first, before ever being listened to.

Most importantly, I have a dream too. When I grow up, I hope to work in a corporation, lead my own meetings—and maybe even be CEO someday. But I continually question if I can truly make it in finance because it is a primarily male-dominated sector. When I search "finance" online and click on the top fifty image hits, I see a man holding a brief-case and sporting slicked-back hair, a fitting black tuxedo, and a slight smirk on his face. Immediately, I begin to think, *Why would anyone hire me when my suit doesn't even fit and I look nothing like the pictures?*

Frankly, I am sick of that self-doubt.

I try to do my best every day. I live by the tenet that hard work means success. So when my bleary eyes flit over to the alarm clock on my bed which mocks me with the "1:00 a.m." on its face because I still have my laptop open to a physics problem I cannot solve, I can't help but feel like there is no point. That I won't fulfill my dreams or ambitions, so I might as well just get my eight hours of sleep. Yet I can't be the only one who questions my purpose in everything I do.

There have to be other girls with tear-stained textbooks, worn-out athletic shoes, or broken instruments wondering what happens after. Because even as they leave their child-hoods with tired minds, bruised shins, and calloused fingers, there is no guaranteed tomorrow.

I knew I could never say all this aloud. To whom would I say it? Who would even want to listen? And even if they did want to hear what I had to say, I could never actually have the courage to look them in the eye and say that we deserve better. I guess I am a little worried I would accidentally agree with them, in fear if they chose to fight back.

So I will always remain thankful to this book for giving me the opportunity to take my time in forming my thoughts and writing them down exactly as I envisioned. To let me say everything I know I could never express aloud. To connect with women who harbor stories and pain we would never realize they possessed if we just walked by them on the street. To meet other writers who are so passionate about their topics and their craft, it makes me feel like I am invincible as long as I have a pencil in my hand.

Writing this book has taught me that we cannot make judgments about the current state of workplace gender inequality without acknowledging the progress the women before us have made. Our history shows it is possible for women to overturn injustice and perform the impossible—which means right now we can only dream what possibilities the future holds.

It also shows that gender inequality is not just a problem for working women alone. All the little girls of the world grow up hearing stories about the pain workplace gender discrimination inflicts on its helpless victims. Little boys are raised by the very same men who treat their female counterparts with disdain. Societal stigma around what a woman is capable of limits men from showing emotions and engaging in more "feminine" tasks or ambitions.

Generation after generation has entered the workforce. Why shouldn't Gen Z—my generation—be the ones to build a workplace that treats all genders the same and allows our children to grow up dreaming without limits?

It terrifies me that people will read this. I have shared parts of my life that strangers will now have, that my closest friends do not even know existed. But I am not the only vulnerable one. All these women shared moments in which they were at their weakest but realized later the inner strength they possessed. When they faced demeaning experiences and were treated as if they did not belong in the workplace, they fought in their own unique ways to prove they did. They may not know each other, but together—separated merely by chapters—they are a shining beacon of light. It hurts to look at them, but it hurts even more to look away. They are a force to be reckoned with.

I doubt the little girls they were would recognize the formidable women they have become. So I don't think I will read this book again right now. I will wait until I become a woman, too, then celebrate how far I have come.

Acknowledgments

I am moved by the support I have received throughout my writing journey. To be completely honest, I almost didn't publish this book. There were so many times when I wanted to quit, wondering if writing this book was even worth it. But your unwavering love and motivation to the finish line inspired me to keep working. Thank you.

To my mom, thank you for embodying the very person I want to be when I grow up. I cannot believe the little girl who used to sleep on your lap while you held her hand and traced the alphabet with her is now an author. You always knew the answer to all my problems, and without your guidance I would truly have been lost.

To my sister, thank you for always making me smile after particularly difficult days trying to cope with the intense workload. You held my hand through both laughter and tears. While this experience may not have gone the way we expected, I am grateful I had you through all the bumps on the ride.

To my father, thank you for being my support system through the pre-sale and telling every single person you knew about this book. You should seriously consider a career in marketing.

To my grandmother, you may not understand English, but I hope you can understand the gratitude and love I pour into these words. Many years ago, you made me promise you would be the first to read my book. Here it is. Thank you for the weekly phone calls reminding me (your favorite grandchild) I can do it.

Thank you to all of this book's interviewees for being vulnerable and sharing your stories with me. I will carry them wherever I go. Your resilience through particularly painful periods of life will not die with you—it will live on in the thousands of young girls' hearts whose hopes you have rekindled. I hope I did your voices justice.

To Mary McCleaft and Genevieve Ventiere, thank you for believing I could really make a difference with my voice and sending encouragement and love my way.

To all my friends, thank you for helping navigate this challenging process with me and reminding me to breathe. I will never forget your excitement in helping me achieve my dreams. I hope one day I can do the same for you all.

To Professor Eric, thank you. I will never forget our first phone call when you told me if I have a story to tell, I should tell it. You believed in me. You took a chance on me when you didn't even know me—not many people would do that.

To my editors Teresa Grabs and Gina Champagne, thank you for patiently answering my countless questions, helping me flesh out my ideas, and getting my manuscript ready for publishing. A huge thank you to the rest of my Manuscripts LLC team whose support and love was endless.

And of course, I thank everyone who pre-ordered *Good but Not Good Enough* and made this publication possible:

Allysa Bertoncini, Dayron Bowers, Nivriti Chaudhuri, Lucy Chen, Saanvi Chigurupati, Ella Cool, April Dailey, Rebecca Davidson, Nicholas D'Souza, Jaya Duraisamy, Natasha Durkins, Ramy Elguindi, Chetan Gautam, Tim Greim,

Kimberly Heathcott, Monish Jain, Sreedevi Kavuturu, Camille Klingen, Susan Koenig, Eric Koester, Chuck Kruelle,

Maycie Kulp, Rajesh Kumbhardare, Smithi Mahendran, Jeejesh Mannambeth, Murali Manohar, Sejal Mashru, Sandip Mazumdar, Mary McCleaft, Scott Mengle, Lauren Mohan, Arun Mohanty, Srividya Muralidhar, Manu Nayak, Koreen Pagano, Suzanne Palmer, Malinda Pratt, Sonia Preta, Jay Punniyakotti, Aditi Purohit, Lucas Respicio, Michael Risch, Nyrka Riskin,

Anna Rorke, Preeta Rout, Sanjib Sahoo, Luis Santiago, Urmi Sen, Lalit Singh, Rhea Singh, Ananya Singhal, Genevieve Ventiere, Aarav Vijay, Neha Yadavilli, Sabrina Yao

Appendix

―

CHAPTER 1

Adams, Abigail. 1776. Braintree: American Yawp. https://www.
americanyawp.com/reader/the-american-revolution/abigail
and-john-adams-converse-on-womens-rights-1776/.

Heyn, Eve. 2023. "It Happened Here: Dr. Elizabeth Blackwell."
Health Matters. Accessed March 17, 2023. https://healthmat-
ters.nyp.org/happened-dr-elizabeth-blackwell/.

History.com Editors. 2017. "'Seneca Falls Convention" History.
com. https://www.history.com/topics/womens-history/sene-
ca-falls-convention.

History, Art & Archives, U.S. House of Representatives. n.d.
"RANKIN, Jeannette." Accessed March 17, 2023. https://history.
house.gov/People/Listing/R/RANKIN,-Jeannette-(R000055)/.

Mandresh, Jason. 2022. "John Adams Responds to the Ladies."
Founder of the Day. October 2022. https://www.founderoft-
heday.com/founder-of-the-day/adams-response.

McFarland, Clair. 2022. "Gap between GOP, Dem Voters in Wyoming Reaches New High." *Cowboy State Daily.* July 6, 2022. https://cowboystatedaily.com/2022/07/06/gap-between-gop-dem-voters-in-wyoming-reaches-new-high/.

Michals, Debra. 2015. "Abigail Adams." National Women's History Museum. https://www.womenshistory.org/education-resources/biographies/abigail-adams.

Rea, Tom. 2014. "The Ambition of Nellie Tayloe Ross." WYO History. https://www.wyohistory.org/encyclopedia/ambition-nellie-tayloe-ross.

US National Archives. n.d. "Woman Suffrage and the 19th Amendment." The US National Archives and Records Administration. https://www.archives.gov/education/lessons/woman-suffrage/.

CHAPTER 2

Anderson, Ashlee. 2018. "Sally Ride." National Women's History Museum. August 16, 2018. Accessed February 17, 2023. https://www.womenshistory.org/education-resources/biographies/sally-ride.

BBC News. 2020. "Ruth Bader Ginsburg in Pictures and Her Own Words." BBC. https://www.bbc.com/news/world-us-canada-54218139.

Blakemore, Erin. 2020. "How Sally Ride Blazed a Trail for Women in Space." *National Geographic.* June 18, 2020. https://www.nationalgeographic.com/history/article/sally-ride-blazed-trail-women-astronauts#.

Contentworks Agency. 2019. "Women Who Rocked the Finance World — Isabel Benham." *Medium* (April). https://content-works.medium.com/women-who-rocked-the-finance-world-isabel-benham-221b1e3363f3.

El Issa, Erin. 2020. "Women and Credit through the Decades: The 1970s." Nerdwallet. July 22, 2020. https://www.nerdwallet.com/article/credit-cards/women-credit-decades-70s.

Equal Credit Opportunity Act (ECOA), 15 U.S.C. § 1691. 1974. https://www.justice.gov/crt/equal-credit-opportunity-act-3. Accessed February 17, 2023.

Goldman, Tom, and Bill Chappell. 2019. "How Bernice Sandler, 'Godmother of Title IX,' Achieved Landmark Discrimination Ban." WHYY. January 10, 2019. https://www.npr.org/2019/01/10/683571958/how-bernice-sandler-godmother-of-title-ix-achieved-landmark-discrimination-ban.

History.com Editors. 2019. "'The Feminine Mystique' by Betty Friedan Is Published." History.com. Updated April 16, 2021. https://www.history.com/this-day-in-history/the-feminine-mystique-by-betty-friedan-is-published.

Muñoz, Jacob. 2021. "The Powerful, Complicated Legacy of Betty Friedan's 'The Feminine Mystique.'" *Smithsonian Magazine.* February 2021. https://www.smithsonianmag.com/smithsonian-institution/powerful-complicated-legacy-betty-friedans-feminine-mystique-180976931/.

Pham, LeBach. 2021. "When Could Women Have a Bank Account? A Short History of Financial Gender Equality and the Financial

Road Ahead." *Spiral* (Blog). April 22, 2021. https://www.spiral.us/blog/when-could-women-have-a-bank-account-a-short-history-of-financial-gender-equality-and-the-financial-road-ahead.

"Sandra Day O'Connor." n.d. Oyez. Accessed February 17, 2023. https://www.oyez.org/justices/sandra_day_oconnor.

"Sandra Day O'Connor." n.d. Sandra Day O'Connor Institute for American Democracy. Accessed February 17, 2023. https://oconnorinstitute.org/civic-programs/oconnor-history/sandra-day-oconnor-policy-archives-research-library/biography/.

Shetterly, Margot. 2017. "Dorothy Vaughan Biography." NASA. https://www.nasa.gov/content/dorothy-vaughan-biography.

Tabacco Mar, Ria. 2020. "Ruth Bader Ginsburg's Fight for Gender Equity Was for All of Us." *SCOTUSblog* (Blog). September 21, 2020. https://www.scotusblog.com/2020/09/ruth-bader-ginsburgs-fight-for-gender-equity-was-for-all-of-us/.

UC Press Blog. n.d. "Ruth Bader Ginsburg's Early Achievements for Gender Equality." *UC Press Blog* (blog), University of California Press. https://www.ucpress.edu/blog/54969/ruth-bader-ginsburgs-early-achievements-for-gender-equality/.

US Department of Health and Human Services. 2021. "Civil Rights Requirements - D. Title IX of the Education Amendments of 1972, 20 U.S.C. 1681 et. seq. (Title IX)." US Department of Health and Human Services. https://www.hhs.gov/civil-rights/

for-individuals/special-topics/needy-families/requirement-d/
index.html.

CHAPTER 4

AAUW. 2020. "Yovino v. Rizo." AAUW. Accessed March 1,
2023. https://www.aauw.org/resources/legal/laf/past-cases/
yovino-v-rizo/.

Bleiweis, Robin. 2021. "Why Salary History Bans Matter To Secur-
ing Equal Pay." March 24, 2021. American Progress. https://
www.americanprogress.org/article/salary-history-bans-mat-
ter-securing-equal-pay/.

CSUSB. 2019. "Latina Math Educator Aileen Rizo: "We can stand
up to injustice." CSUSB. October 1, 2019. https://www.csusb.
edu/inside/article/508397/latina-math-educator-aileen-rizo-
we-can-stand-injustice/.

Depaulo, Lisa. 2018. "Inside Aileen Rizo's Fight For Equal Pay."
Bazaar. July 24, 2018. https://www.harpersbazaar.com/culture/
politics/a22518299/aileen-rizo-equal-pay-case-california-state-
assembly/.

Hutchins, Gudrun. n.d. "The Long Road to Pay Equity: After 8 Years
Aileen Rizo Finally Wins Her Case in Court." AAUW. Accessed
March 1, 2023. https://bennington-vt.aauw.net/1344-2/.

Minter, Harriet. 2016. "#Freekesha but Don't Forget the Other
Women Silenced by Fear." *The Guardian.* https://amp.theguard-
ian.com/women-in-leadership/2016/feb/24/freekesha-wom-
en-fear-sexual-harassment-money.

PowHer NY. 2014. "7 Women Shortchanged: Personal Stories of the Gender Pay Gap." PowHer New York. http://www.powherny. org/2014/04/06/7-women-shortchanged-personal-stories-of-the-gender-pay-gap/.

CHAPTER 5

Gabrielle, Natasha. 2022. "58% of Families Plan to Spend Over $10,000 on Child Care Costs in 2022." The Ascent.

https://www.fool.com/the-ascent/personal-finance/articles/58-of-families-plan-to-spend-over-10000-on-child-care-costs-in-2022/.

Kurtzleben, Danielle. 2015. "Lots Of Other Countries Mandate Paid Leave. Why Not The U.S.?" npr. https://www.npr.org/sections/itsallpolitics/2015/07/15/422957640/lots-of-other-countries-mandate-paid-leave-why-not-the-us.

Schochet, Leila. 2019. "The Child Care Crisis Is Keeping Women Out of the Workforce." CAP. https://www.americanprogress. org/article/child-care-crisis-keeping-women-workforce/.

US Department of Labor. 2023. "Fact Sheet #28: The Family and Medical Leave Act." WHD. https://www.dol.gov/agencies/whd/fact-sheets/28-fmla.

CHAPTER 6

Mohr, Tara. 2014. "Why Women Don't Apply for Jobs Unless They're 100% Qualified." *Harvard Business Review*, August

2014. https://hbr.org/2014/08/why-women-dont-apply-for-jobs-unless-theyre-100-qualified.

Slyter, Kirsten. 2021. "Why Is Childcare So Expensive? 7 Factors at Play." Rasmussen University (blog). October 25 2021. https://www.rasmussen.edu/degrees/education/blog/why-is-child-care-so-expensive/.

Taketa, Kristen. 2023. "California's child care aid misses hundreds of thousands of families who need it." *The San Diego Union-Tribune*, January 8, 2023. https://www.sandiegouniontribune.com/news/education/story/2023-01-08/california-subsidized-child-care-crisis-families-aid.

CHAPTER 8

Bifoss, Bailey. 2019. "Who's The Boss? How Managers Can Handle Gender Bias From Their Own Subordinates." Fisher Phillips. June 3, 2019. https://www.fisherphillips.com/news-insights/who-s-the-boss-how-managers-can-handle-gender-bias-from-their-own-subordinates.html.

Mann, Dhar. 2020. "Male Boss Treats Female Employees Unfair At Work, He Lives To Regret It." Dhar Mann. December 1, 2020. 8:57. https://www.youtube.com/watch?v=tnYGNDitdiA.

Melindasleadership. 2018. "Women In Insurance – A History – The 1980s." Melindasleadership. August 27, 2018. https://melindasleadership.com/2018/08/27/women-in-insurance-a-history-the-1980s/#.

Ross, Hailey, and Jason Woleben. 2020. "Female Insurance Leaders Work against Odds to Open Doors for Oher Women." S&P Global Market Intelligence. November 17, 2020. Accessed December 26, 2022. https://www.spglobal.com/marketintelligence/en/news-insights/latest-news-headlines/female-insurance-leaders-work-against-odds-to-open-doors-for-other-women-60699653.

STEMconnector. 2017. "Women in Insurance: Leading to Action." STEMconnector and MWM. 2017. Accessed December 26, 2022. https://www.acord.org/docs/default-source/research-public/women_in_insurance_2018.pdf.

CHAPTER 9

Hewlett, Sylvia, Melinda Marshall, and Laura Sherbin. 2013. "Looking for Innovation in All the Wrong Places." *Stanford Social Innovation Review*, September 2013. https://ssir.org/articles/entry/looking_for_innovation_in_all_the_wrong_places.

Janjuha-Jivraj, Shaheena. 2023. "The Daddy Dilemma, Why Fatherhood Is Still a Penalty for Men's Careers." *Forbes*. May 16, 2023. https://www.forbes.com/sites/shaheenajanjuhajivrajeurope/2023/05/16/the-daddy-dilemma-why-fatherhood-is-still-a-penalty-for-mens-careers/?sh=51cbaf2341bc.

Sinclair, Samantha. 2021. "Bystander Reactions to Workplace Incivility: The Role of Gender and Discrimination Claims." NIH. https://www.ncbi.nlm.nih.gov/pmc/articles/PMC7957849/.

CHAPTER 10

Pew Research Center. 2018. "The Data on Women Leaders." September 13, 2018. https://www.pewresearch.org/social-trends/fact-sheet/the-data-on-women-leaders/.

Szakal, Arpad. 2019. "Is Gender Still Holding Women Back in the Aviation Industry?" Royal Aeronautical Society. Accessed November 27, 2022. https://www.aerosociety.com/news/is-gender-still-holding-women-back-in-the-aviation-industry/.

CHAPTER 12

Adichie, Chimamanda Ngozi. 2013. "We Should All Be Feminists." TEDx. April 12, 2013. 30:15. https://www.youtube.com/watch?v=hg3umXU_qWc.

Essig, Elena, and Richard Soparnot. 2019. "Re-thinking Gender Inequality in the Workplace—A Framework from the Male Perspective." *M@n@gement* 22, no. 3 (July): 373–410. https://www.cairn-int.info/journal-management-2019-3-page-373.htm.

Kimmel, Michael. 2015. "Why Gender Equality Is Good for Everyone — Men Included." TED Talk. October 6, 2015. 15:58. https://www.youtube.com/watch?v=7n9IOHoNvyY.

Menengage. 2020. "7 Ways Men Can be Better Allies for Gender Equality." Menengage Alliance. July 13, 2020. https://menengage.unfpa.org/en/news/7-ways-men-can-be-better-allies-gender-equality.

State Government of Victoria. 2021. "Gender Inequality Affects Everyone." Victorian Government: AU. https://www.vic.gov. au/gender-inequality-affects-everyone/.